24, 5-7

The World of

WILLIAM PENN

by Genevieve Foster

illustrated by
the author

CHARLES SCRIBNER'S SONS
NEW YORK

24256

CONTENTS

being a friend of King James II and why Pennsylvania was taken from him by William and Mary.

PART ONE

The life story of

WILLIAM PENN

1660–1684

telling how he became a Quaker

and why and how the King of England

CHARLES II

gave him the colony of

PENNSYLVANIA

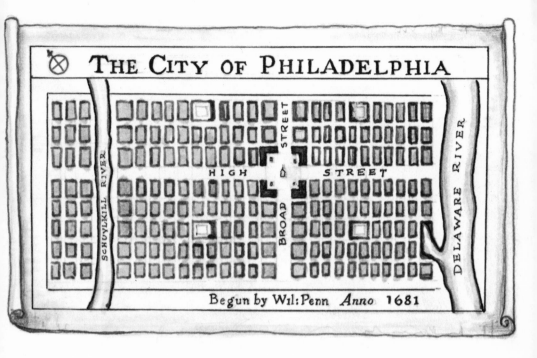

THE CITY OF PHILADELPHIA

SCHUYLKILL RIVER

BROAD STREET

HIGH STREET

DELAWARE RIVER

Begun by Wil: Penn *Anno* 1681

FOR WILLIAM PENN the last few days of October, 1682, must have been the happiest, most exciting days of his life. He was here in America, here at last in his own new land of Pennsylvania, which had been given to him by the King of England more than a year ago. All that year had been spent making plans and preparations to leave. But now he was here, seeing with his own eyes the wonderful, wooded land along the Delaware River and walking through the tiny settlement that was to become the city of Philadelphia.

He had planned to make it a "green country town" with

9

spacious lawns and wide straight streets. The men he had sent ahead to lay it out had followed his plan so well that he was completely satisfied. His broad, kind face was shining with pleasure as they escorted him along the wide street that ran straight as an arrow from the Delaware River to the Schuylkill River two miles to the west. Halfway there they turned up another wide street a mile long running north and south.

Full of energy, William Penn went striding along, commenting, praising, looking to right and left. Autumn leaves were falling and the trees were golden yellow. Here and there surveyors could be seen measuring off plots of land for future houses and gardens.

Already ten small new houses had been built along a narrow road leading down to an old tavern, long used by fur trappers and Indian traders. This tavern stood on the sandy edge of a pond, which formed a natural harbor opening into the Delaware. This is where William Penn had first stepped ashore in Philadelphia. He had come there up the river on a small boat.

The large ship, the "Welcome," on which he had sailed from England, had ended its voyage farther down the river at New Castle, Delaware. There, after almost two months on the ocean, the exhausted passengers had landed, thankful to be alive. Thirty-one had died of smallpox on the way over, so only about seventy were left of those who started out from England. All of them, like their devoted leader, William Penn, were members of the Society of Friends, usually called Quakers.

Pennsylvania had been planned as a colony especially for the Quakers. It would be a place in which they could live free from the persecution which they suffered in England, where the Quakers, like others who did not belong to the Church of England, were punished because of their religion. They were fined, imprisoned, tortured and even killed for failing to obey the orders of the king, who because he was king was also head of the church.

Why then had this king been willing to give the rich land of Pennsylvania to one of those stubborn Quakers who refused to obey his orders?

The story of that amazing gift begins twenty-two years earlier, in the year 1660, when Charles II, known as the "Merry Monarch," became king of England and William Penn, sixteen, had not yet thought of becoming a Quaker.

THIS IS CHARLES II, known as the "Merry Monarch" for his happy-go-lucky way of life. Much of his time was spent gambling with his friends and making love to the ladies.

Until he became king, however, he had slight reason to be merry. For fourteen years he had been a refugee drifting around Europe, with no home, no money and little hope of ever getting back to England, much less of being called back by Parliament to be made king.

His father, Charles I, had waged a war against Parliament, lost the war and as a result had been condemned to death and beheaded. After that, Oliver Cromwell, commander of Parliament's army, became ruler of England. He was honest and capable but he was a Puritan and his rule was very strict. Soon after he died, the king's friends came back into power and sent a joyful invitation to Charles II to return. One of those friends who went to Europe to escort the new king home was William Penn's father, Admiral William Penn, a commander in the British navy. On board ship coming home, he was knighted by the now merry monarch and became SIR William Penn.

The new king's entry into London was a glorious occasion. Streets were strewn with flowers, bells were ringing and people shouting for joy. The coronation procession was even more glorious and glittering. Young William Penn went with his father, Sir William, to view it from the window of a private house which the procession was to pass on its way from the Tower of London to Westminster Abbey. The Penns had been invited there with a few friends, including a neighbor, Mr. Samuel Pepys, who wrote that night in his diary about the splendid spectacle: "So glorious was the show with gold and silver that we were unable to look at it, our eyes at last being so much overcome. Both the King and [his brother] the Duke of York took notice of us at the window."

That was the crowning moment of the day for Sir William Penn. To be noticed by the king and his brother as they rode by! And to have them also see his handsome son standing beside him.

William was now in his first year at Oxford University. He was a very good student—even a bit too studious and serious-minded, his father may have thought. He himself was a hearty sea-going man, more ready to eat, drink and be merry than to read a book. However, William was a splendid lad, and Sir William had no doubt that as soon as he graduated from Oxford, he would step into some high position at the king's court.

ON A FOGGY MARCH DAY IN 1662, young William
Penn was walking slowly toward his home on Tower Hill,
near the Tower of London, dreading with every step the
moment that he had to face his father. He, William Penn,
in his second year at Oxford, had been expelled! Not even
being the son of Sir William, who was a friend of the king,
had saved him from this shocking disgrace.

Yet he was not ashamed of what he had done. He had

simply refused to go along with certain rules and regulations about religion laid down by the University, rules which he and his group of friends believed were unfair.

Just as he feared, his hot-tempered father raged and stormed and beat him, and, except for his mother, would have turned him out of the house. Later, when the angry man cooled off, he decided that France might be the place for William to finish his education and get some new ideas about life.

One night, shortly before William left, Samuel Pepys wrote in his diary that he "had Sir W. Penn and son William to my house for dinner." They dined on venison. Over two years later, when William returned from France, he was, according to Mr. Pepys, "a most modish person," dressed in the latest French fashion, with ruffles, ribbons and a curled wig. He spoke perfect French and had also perfected his Latin and Greek. All that he needed now, thought his happy father, was some training in the law to prepare him for a high place in the royal government.

So in February, 1665, William Penn entered a law school known as Lincoln's Inn, which was toward the opposite end of London from his home on Tower Hill. As he went back and forth he saw the result of recent laws, passed by Parliament and signed by the king, which were intended to stamp out all opposition to the Church of England. No preacher of any other church was allowed to hold a meeting within five miles of any town. William often saw meetings being broken up by the police, worshippers arrested and dragged off to jail, while bystanders yelled and jeered and pelted them with stones. Among those who suffered most were a group known as Quakers.

That summer William's days at law school were suddenly cut short by a deadly disease that broke out in London. This horrible disease, known as the Great Plague, was so contagious that all schools were closed. The poor people in the slums were boarded up in their houses to keep the plague from spreading. Those who caught it died so fast that wagonloads of dead bodies had to be buried together in huge pits.

During that dreadful time, William Penn was amazed to see the Quakers going about taking food to the poor, caring for the sick and gathering up the dead. He wondered how they could do it. Where did they find the courage? What could be the source of their strength?

OLD ST. PAUL'S CATHEDRAL

The CIT

THE THAMES

ONLY A YEAR AFTER THE PLAGUE came another disaster, the awful fire of London, which raged for five days and left over half of the city in ruins. It started in a baker's shop at the south side of London Bridge, which soon became

18

an arch of fire spanning the river. The flames were blown westward, so the houses on Tower Hill were spared, though neither Sir William Penn nor his neighbor Samuel Pepys had been sure of it. Having put their chests of gold coins in the cellar, they dug pits in the garden in which to bury their valuable papers as well as Sir William's wine and the Parmesan cheese of Mr. Samuel Pepys.

According to Mr. Pepys's diary dated September 2, 1666, the fire had started the night before. He rose early that morning and went with a friend "to the waterside and there got a boat [going] so near to the fire as we could for the smoke. When we could endure it no more, we went to a little ale house and there staid till it was almost dark and saw the fire grow up the hill of the city in a most horrid malicious bloody flame. The horrid noise the flames made and the cracking of houses in their ruin was enough to put us out of our wits."

September 7: "Up by five o'clock and blessed be God! All is well. I home late to Sir W. Pen's who did give me a bed; but without curtains or hanging, all being down. I did sleep pretty well; but still both sleep and waking had a fear of fire in my heart."

During those five awful days while London was burning, King Charles rode about the streets doing whatever he could to help in fighting the fire. Then almost before the ashes had cooled off, he asked his royal surveyor to present plans for rebuilding the city.

THIS IS SIR CHRISTOPHER WREN, the architect, or royal surveyor. He must have been working day and night, for in less than a week he arrived at the palace with a roll of plans for the king's approval. His idea, as he pointed out, was to do away with the narrow crooked lanes and small filthy courts of old London and turn it into a beautiful city with broad avenues and spacious squares. It would be safer as well as more beautiful.

One reason the fire spread so fast had to do with the narrow streets. Some were so narrow that if two wagons happened to meet, one would have to back up to let the other pass. And the upper stories of the wooden houses extended so far beyond the lower ones that neighbors could actually reach across and shake hands.

Charles II was delighted with Christopher Wren's plan, but it could not be carried out. The owners of the burnt-out property would not give up their right to rebuild their houses and shops on the old foundations.

Over fifty of the churches that had been destroyed in the fire were rebuilt by Christopher Wren. The one for which he is most famous is St. Paul's Cathedral. It took thirty-five years after the first stone was laid until the cathedral was finished. During all that time Sir Christopher kept constant watch over every detail of the construction. Several times a week, passersby might see him being pulled up in a basket to the great dome—which when completed would be the crown on the cathedral of St. Paul.

Castle in Ireland

WILLIAM PENN WAS NOT IN LONDON during the great fire. He was in Ireland, where he had gone to look after his father's property. Charles II had just given Sir William 7,000 acres of Irish land, including a castle and a fort not far from the city of Cork. Sir William received excellent reports of his son as manager of the estate and also of his success as an army officer in helping to put down a revolt.

This is a copy of a portrait of young William Penn in

armor. It is dated 1666, when he was thinking he might like to be given full command of his father's fort. A year later, all his interest in being a soldier was gone. And Sir William was notified that on September 3, 1667, his son had been imprisoned in Cork with a group of Quakers.

Impossible! thought that old navy commander who had fought so many battles for England. How could a son of his be joined in any way with those strange Quakers, so peculiar that they did not even believe in war. But it was true.

This is what happened. One day, William went to Cork, dressed as usual in a fancy suit with ruffles at his wrists and a sword at his side. He stepped into a small shop owned by a Quaker lady. After introducing himself, he mentioned that he had lived in Ireland once before when he was a young boy and that he had then heard a certain Quaker preacher speak. He had never forgotten it, he said, and would go far to hear him again.

"Thee need not leave Cork to hear him," said the little lady. "He is to speak tomorrow night at a Friends Meeting."

That meeting was a turning point in William Penn's life. Suddenly, many questions that had been puzzling him for years seemed to be answered. He heard of an inner power that came to each person directly from God—a kind of Inner Light to guide him through life.

After that he went to more Quaker meetings, most of them quiet ones, with no minister and no spoken words except when one of the congregation was moved to speak.

One day a soldier burst in and broke up the meeting. William Penn jumped to his feet, seized the soldier by the neck and was about to pitch him down the stairs, when the Friends stopped him; they did not believe in violence. The soldier left but was soon back with reinforcements. Nineteen Quakers were then arrested and marched off to prison. There the officer in charge took one look at William Penn with his ruffles and sword and dismissed him. Compared to the others in their flat hats and somber gray clothes, he looked like a bird of paradise in a flock of doves. He was no Quaker!

"Indeed I am a Friend," protested William Penn and insisted on remaining with the others.

Just before he stepped through the prison door, he unbuckled his sword and handed it to a bystander, declaring he would never again carry arms. From prison he wrote to the king's lieutenant and got all of the prisoners set free.

Almost the same day he received a sharp command from

his father to report home at once. Sir William had moved from London shortly after the fire to a large house in the country. So this time William was not going home to Tower Hill, nor did he have to face his father alone. He had brought a young Quaker friend to help him through the first meeting. The angry father kept his temper until he had his son alone. Then he raged and stormed until he was out of words. For the next few weeks he saw his son as little as possible and said almost nothing to him.

William Penn was truly sorry to offend his father, who had always been his hero. As a little boy he had been so happy whenever his father came home from sea, and so proud of him when he won a great victory.

Now, however, nothing was so important to him as the wonderful new way of living that he had discovered. Day after day he went to Friends meetings in London. And soon he began to preach himself, he was so eager to have others enjoy the "peace of mind" he felt at last.

In time, one of the meetings was broken up by the police; Sir William was notified. And he, having reached the frayed end of his endurance, promptly ordered that Quaker son of his to pack up his belongings and begone!

CHRISTMAS DAY, 1668, WILLIAM PENN sat alone shivering in a small unheated room in the Tower of London, eating the grim everyday dinner served to prisoners. It was just two weeks since he had been arrested and put in prison. He was arrested because of a book which he had written telling why Quakers could not accept a certain belief held by the Church of England. The printer of the book was also put into prison because he had published the book without first obtaining a license from the bishop of London.

There was no freedom of speech in England, just as there was no freedom of religion under that so-called merry monarch, Charles II. However, the young man in prison was the son of the king's friend, Sir William Penn. And Sir William was wealthy enough to loan the king money, which he was always needing to maintain his merry way of life. So the king sent a bishop to tell Sir William's son that if he would take back what he had written in the book, he would be released. Otherwise he would be a prisoner for life. William Penn flatly refused. His conscience was not for sale.

Later, however, he did write a pamphlet denying a belief that his enemies falsely claimed was to be found in his book. And so, after nine miserable months spent in the Tower of London, he was set free. The officer in charge received an order signed by the king to deliver the prisoner into the custody of Sir W. Penn, who immediately sent his son back to Ireland. William was gone a year, looking after the estate and collecting some rents that were due. Hardly had he returned to London than he was arrested again.

This time it was for "disturbing the peace" by preaching in the street. He had begun by speaking to a small group of Friends standing in front of their meeting house, which had been boarded up by the police. He spoke so well that a crowd gathered to listen. In no time, he and another Friend were arrested, charged with "disturbing the peace" and brought to trial before a jury of twelve men.

It turned out to be a noisy trial, with both sides interrupting and insulting each other, while the audience stamped and clapped as if they were watching a cock fight.

William Penn pleaded "not guilty" to the charge. And knowing the law, he argued his own case. The judge (or recorder, as he was called) ordered the jury to bring in a verdict of GUILTY. More than that, he threatened to have them locked up with nothing to eat or drink until they did as they were told. To threaten the jury in this way was common practice in that very merry England of Charles II.

William Penn would have none of it. He challenged the judge and encouraged the jury to defy the judge and disobey his orders. He reminded them of the right to fair trial guaranteed to all Englishmen by the Magna Carta, that ancient charter of English rights and privileges.

"Ye are Englishmen," he told them. "Mind your privileges! Give not away your rights!"

"Nor will we ever!" shouted four of the twelve men who had stood firm from the beginning.

The other eight were more fearful. But at last they too

dared to return the verdict NOT GUILTY. So those twelve men, supported by William Penn's courage, made this trial a landmark in the history of English justice.

William Penn and his friend, however, did not go free. They were unjustly fined for contempt of court and then put in prison for refusing to pay the fine. This time William was put into Newgate Prison, a loathsome, filthy place crowded with all kinds of criminals. He himself had the inner strength to endure it, but he was concerned about his father, who was then very ill and not expected to live.

William wrote him a long letter, urging him not to worry, not to pay the fine, that all would work out for the best. No great good was ever gained without suffering.

Sir William was happy with the letter. Certainly that son of his was no weakling. It took courage to suffer and stand up as he did for what he believed. Sir William gladly paid the fine. And William was there with his father on the sixteenth of September, 1670, when the old commander died. Before that, knowing that he had not long to live, Sir William had written to the king and received his promise and also that of his brother, the Duke of York, "to continue their favor toward his son."

IT WAS AN AUGUST MORNING during the following
summer. On a wharf at the mouth of the Thames River, a
small group of Friends were watching a ship leaving for
America. Among them were William Penn and Guli, a beautiful young woman, whose full name was Gulielma Springett
and who was to become Mrs. William Penn the following
spring. They had come to see the most important Friend in

31

England off on his first visit to the colonies in America.

He was George Fox, who had founded the Society of Friends—the first person ever to be called a Quaker. He began to preach his new faith in 1647 when William Penn was three years old. Two years later, when he was arrested for preaching, he rebuked the justice of the peace, saying, "Thee should tremble at the word of the Lord."

The officer laughed at the idea of trembling. And since to tremble was to quake, he scornfully called the young preacher a "quaker." That is how the name originated.

George Fox was so sincere and his message so appealing that in a short time he gained many followers. They in turn were eager to act as missionaries. By the time Charles II became king, there were about forty thousand Quakers in England and Ireland and the first missionaries had already arrived in the Puritan colony of Massachusetts. The people of Boston showed them no mercy. They cut off their ears, bored holes in their tongues and whipped them out of town. Nevertheless, Quaker missionaries continued to go to the colonies. They traveled up and down the coast from Rhode Island to Virginia, gaining followers and setting up meeting places.

George Fox spent two years on his visit to America. On

his return home, William and Guli Penn were at the harbor to welcome their dear friend. The traveler looked worn and thin, but he had good news. The Quakers, he said, were surviving and increasing in the colonies in spite of persecution. And yet how wonderful it would be if they could have a colony of their own! Why not?

Massachusetts had been given to the Puritans. Lord Baltimore had been granted Maryland as a refuge for English Catholics. True, there was no land left along the coast, but north of Maryland along the Delaware River there was much deeply wooded land inhabited only by the Indians.

Up until then, William Penn had been so busy writing books, preaching throughout England and even going on a mission to Holland and Germany that he had not thought much about the New World. From now on he became more and more interested. First of all, in New Jersey.

About that time, because of his knowledge of the law, he was asked to settle a dispute between two Quakers who had purchased the western half of New Jersey from the previous owner. After settling the dispute, William Penn was appointed with two others to govern the colony. They wrote a plan of government which guaranteed three freedoms lacking in England: freedom of speech, freedom of religion and impartial justice for every citizen under the law.

A pamphlet describing West New Jersey was circulated among the Friends and in 1677, when the first shipload of settlers sailed for the new colony, most of them were Quakers. On the shore of the Delaware River, they built the town of Burlington, after buying rights to the land from the Indians. West New Jersey soon became a thriving community, but it was too small to hold all the Quakers who needed a safe place to live. Directly across the Delaware River, however, was that deeply wooded land north of Maryland, inhabited only by the Indians. What about that? thought William Penn.

How could he persuade the king to give him that land? What excuse could the king give to his bishops for making such a present to a Quaker? The only reason could be the king's friendship with his father. In fact, there was the answer! Sir William had loaned Charles II 16,000 pounds that had never been repaid. The king, he believed, would be willing to give him, Sir William's son, this land in payment of that debt. And he was right. Charles II signed a bill authorizing the charter.

ON MARCH 4, 1681, THE ROYAL CHARTER was presented to William Penn Esquire, making him sole proprietor of a vast tract of land in America, to be known as Pennsylvania. For this, the said owner was to pay the king a fee of "two beaver skins to be delivered at our castle of Windsor on the first day of January every year" plus one fifth of any gold and silver that might be found in the land.

Why it was named Pennsylvania is told by William Penn in this part of a letter written that night to a friend in Ireland.

DEAR FRIEND:

My true love in the Lord salutes thee . . . know that this day my country was confirmed to me under the Great Seal of England, by the name of Pennsylvania; a name the King would give it in honor of my father. I chose New Wales; when the Secretary, a Welshman, refused to have it [I proposed] Sylvania and they added Penn to it. I much opposed it and went to the King to have it struck out for I feared lest it should be looked on as a vanity in me, and not as a respect to my father, whom he [the King] often mentions with praise.

It is a clear and just thing and God will, I believe, bless it and make it the seed of a nation.

Thy true friend,

WM. PENN.

SYLVANIA, the name which William Penn proposed, is the Latin word for woods. As he also knew Greek, he combined "philos," the Greek word for love, with "adelphos," meaning brother, into Philadelphia, City of Brotherly Love.

Now with the Charter in his hand, William Penn began busy months of preparation to make his "Holy Experiment," as he called it, a success. His desk was piled high with maps and papers. He worked every minute, advertising the colony among the Quakers; arranging grants of land to those who wished to buy; designing the new government; drawing plans for the new city; selecting a surveyor to lay it out; and appointing a governor and other officers to go ahead and take charge of affairs until he could join them.

William Markham, his cousin, who was to act as governor, carried a friendly letter of introduction to Lord Baltimore in neighboring Maryland. He found that gentleman already disturbed about how far south this new colony of Pennsylvania was to extend and where the actual boundary line lay.

The original grant to William Penn was twenty-eight million acres, but none of it was on the Atlantic coast. To correct this, he had joined with eleven other Quakers to purchase East New Jersey. Added to West New Jersey, that gave them all of the New Jersey coastline.

Still he had only one side of Delaware Bay, which was the important outlet to the sea for Philadelphia. To correct this, he purchased from the king's brother, James, the duke of York, the land which is now the state of Delaware. This last purchase was made in August 1682, just before William Penn was to leave England.

Dear Letitia *My Dear Spring* *Dear Bill*

THE PENN FAMILY, William, Guli and their three children, lived in a country home in Sussex south of London. It was a large house with many rooms and many servants to care for it. One August night when the entire household was asleep, there must have been somewhere in that dark and silent house a candle burning and the tiny scratching of a quill pen. William Penn would have been found at his desk, writing a farewell letter to his beloved Guli, telling her how much he loved her.

38

At the end of August he was leaving for America. Guli was expecting another baby, so she was not going with him. He feared he might never see her again. No voyage across the stormy Atlantic was without danger. In case Guli should be left alone without his help in the years to come he was writing long careful instructions about bringing up the children.

He counseled her first of all to train them to love one another; to spare no cost in their education; to have them tutored at home rather than sent to school; and when they were old enough, to see that each one married a worthy person. Their father was looking far ahead.

Springett, the oldest, was only seven. Letitia was four and William Junior was two. To each one of them he wrote a separate letter much like this one:

My Dear Springett:

Be good, learn to fear God, avoid evil, love thy book, be kind to thy brother and sister and God will bless thee and I will exceedingly love thee. Farewell dear child.

Thy dear father
Wm. Penn.

ALL THE FAREWELLS HAD BEEN SAID, his luggage and servants were aboard ship and by the first of September William Penn was on his way to America. Two months later, on October 27, 1682, just as a huge red sun was setting behind the town of New Castle, Delaware, his ship, the "Welcome," dropped anchor in the bay. New Castle was the most important town on Delaware Bay and part of the territory William Penn had purchased from the duke of York.

A welcoming ceremony had been planned for the new proprietor. The night was spent aboard ship, but next morning as he stepped ashore a delegation was there to meet him,

including the governor, surveyor and land commissioners he had sent over and also an attorney representing His Royal Highness, the Duke of York. They escorted him with great formality to the fort. There he was first handed a piece of turf with a twig in it, to show that he owned the land, and then a bowl of water from the Delaware to show that he also owned the water. Then the key to the fort was presented.

People from all over the region had come for the ceremony, Indians as well as Dutch and Swedish settlers. A representative of the Swedes, who had been the first people to settle this part of the bay, made a speech, promising the new owner to "love, serve and obey."

Later in the day William Penn and the Friends went back to the ship and continued up the river to the Swedish town of Upland, which he renamed Chester. There they spent the night. Early next morning on a small boat he was on his way to the site where his City of Brotherly Love was being laid out and where he was delighted to see how closely the surveyor and land commisioners had followed his plans.

PENNSBURY MANOR was the next place he was eager to see. This was to be his home, a home in the country for Guli and the children, a large three-storied red brick house with many rooms not unlike the one they had in England. It was to be surrounded by flower gardens and herb gardens and there would be stone steps leading down to the river. It was on a vast tract of land, about twenty-five miles up the river from Philadelphia.

1 Manor House
2 Kitchen
3 Bake and Brew House
4 Smoke House
5 Wood Shed
6 Office
7 Ice House
8 Tool House
9 Stables
10 Barge

Pennsbury Manor

William Markham had purchased the land that summer from the Indians. For it he had paid 2,000 feet of wampum (Indian money) plus 300 guilders (Dutch money). To that he had added twenty blankets, twenty kettles, ten yards of woolen cloth, guns, coats, shirts, stockings, hoes, knives, pipes, combs, scissors, tobacco, rum, cider and beer, until the Indians were entirely satisfied with the bargain.

That the Indians should be satisfied was most important to William Penn. Just because the king of England had given him this land of Pennsylvania was no reason in his mind for disregarding the Indians, whose home it had been long before the white man came. Unless the English settlers treated the Indians fairly, how could the English expect the Indians to treat them as neighbors and friends?

DO UNTO OTHERS AS YOU WOULD HAVE THEM
DO UNTO YOU

was the Golden Rule on which his Holy Experiment was based.

Word had sped like the wind through the Indian villages that the Great White Sachem was here! For many moons the Indians had been expecting him. He had sent them a letter saying he would come and speaking to them of the Great Spirit, whom he called by a strange short name. Here is part of William Penn's letter:

MY FRIENDS:

There is one great God and power that hath made the world and all things therein to whom you and I and all people owe their being . . . this great God hath written His law in our hearts by which we are taught to love, help and be good to one another . . . Now the King of the country where I live hath given unto me a great province (in your parts of the world). But I desire to enjoy it with your love and consent, that we may always live together as neighbors and friends.

I am your loving friend,
WILLIAM PENN.

How much of a friend would he prove to be, the Indians wondered, now that he was here? They had not long to wonder. Very soon, before the moon of the long frost, an invitation came to the sachems to meet William Penn and make what was to become a famous treaty of peace.

The meeting place was to be at Shackamaxon, near the new
town he was building, under the branches of a wide spreading elm. As the sachems and braves approached the great elm,
carrying their bows and arrows and tomahawks, they saw a
small group of white men standing there completely unarmed. Not one of them wore a sword or carried a gun. The
one wearing a blue sash they identified immediately as the
sachem they had come to meet.

That is why William Penn had worn it. He knew that the
Indians would expect a chief to have some mark to distin-
guish him from his followers. He wished in every way he
could to respect the customs of the Indians.

After smoking the calumet, or peace pipe, together, the
Indians and Quakers spoke of peace first and then about the
land. When the Indians wished time to deliberate regarding
the land, William Penn was not impatient. He knew that
each chief took council with all the men of his nation, young

and old, and was moved to act "by the breath of his people." As to their friendship, that, the Indians assured him, would endure "as long as the sun and the moon gave light."

The conversation was carried on through an interpreter. As he listened, William Penn thought the words of the Indian language had great sweetness and rhythm and within a year had added it to the other languages which he spoke. One Indian word he must have learned that very day was the word *onus* which meant "quill." The Indians knew that the white men used a goose quill for a pen. Since they themselves never used a pen, they had no exact word for it. *Onus* was as near as they could come to the name of their new friend, Pen, or Penn. Later, in the months to come, as he visited in their villages, ate with them, joined in their games and sports, he became very dear to them. They called him "Brother Onus."

They gave him a belt of wampum, showing the Indian and the white man clasping hands to commemorate the Great Treaty. Eighty years later, the famous French author, Voltaire, wrote of it as the "only treaty between those nations [the Indians] and the Christians which was never sworn to and never broken."

THE GREAT LAW, OR CONSTITUTION, for Pennsylvania had been written by William Penn before he left England. Although in the Charter the king had given him almost absolute power to govern the colony, William Penn gave that power away to the people. For he believed that the government should belong to the people. They should make their own laws. So sincerely did he believe this that he stayed away from the first assembly held in Chester on the fourth of December, when the Great Law was presented to the people for their approval. He wanted them to feel free to make whatever changes they saw fit.

Three days later William Penn came, approved their few

slight changes, and the Great Law was enacted.

First of all it guaranteed freedom of religion, freedom of speech and fair trial. It also provided that:

All resident taxpayers should have the right to vote.

Every child over twelve years of age should be taught some some trade or useful occupation.

There should be only two crimes for which a man could be put to death, murder and treason. In Massachusetts and Connecticut there were at least fourteen acts punishable by death. And over two hundred in England, where a man could be hanged for stealing a sheep or even a loaf of bread.

Every prison should be made a workshop where a prisoner could be taught a trade and reformed. Never before in the history of the world had anyone proposed that instead of merely locking a man up, he should be given the chance to learn a new way of life. For this idea, William Penn certainly deserves to be remembered.

It was about a week after the Great Law had been approved that William Penn went to Maryland for his first meeting with Lord Baltimore. He was hoping, in a friendly conversation, to settle any uncertainty about the border line between Pennsylvania and Maryland.

After a few words it was plain to see that this was impossible. The way the two charters had been written was not at all clear. The land had never been properly surveyed. And no accurate maps had ever been drawn. Much guesswork had resulted in wide disagreement.

And it was not just one border that Lord Baltimore was upset about. He questioned William Penn's right to the land along Delaware Bay. True, he realized that it had been purchased by Mr. Penn from the duke of York, but did the duke of York have the right to sell it? Did he really own it? That was the question. Everyone knew how the duke had acquired it. It had been part of the New Netherlands, which had been taken by the English after winning a war against the Dutch.

Charles II had then given the land to his brother and changed the name to New York. But what Lord Baltimore wanted to know was, when did the Dutch settle on the Delaware River? Was it before 1632? If not, then the land belonged to him. For the Maryland Charter was given to his father in 1632.

Since neither one had the answer to that question, it was obvious that the problem would have to be settled by the king's Privy Council. Lord Baltimore and William Penn each sent the council a report stating his side of the argument. A year went by, and since nothing had been heard from the council, both men decided to present their case in person. Lord Baltimore left for England first. William Penn sailed from Philadelphia in August, 1684, almost exactly two years from the time he had left England for his great adventure in America.

The following summer it was decreed by the council that the land between the Delaware River and Chesapeake Bay should be divided between Maryland and Pennsylvania. Before the other border line had been decided upon, serious trouble arose in the English government that so affected the life of William Penn that it was to be fifteen years before he could return to Pennsylvania.

PART TWO

introducing

Three French Explorers

MARQUETTE and JOLLIET

who discovered the Mississippi in

1672

LA SALLE

who named the river valley Louisiana

for the King of France in

1682

the year that Philadelphia was founded

Marquette

Jolliet

La Salle

55

NEW FRANCE WAS THE NAME FOR CANADA in the time of William Penn. Quebec, its capital city, had been founded by a French explorer just a year after the first permanent English settlement was made at Jamestown, Virginia. Along with the French explorers and fur traders, Jesuit missionaries had come out to New France, to work among the Indians and teach them the Catholic religion.

56

All European explorers still held the hope that Columbus had had of finding a waterway that would lead through to China. When the French heard the Indians tell of a wide mysterious river in the west, they began to hope that this great river, which the Indians called the Mississippi, might be the long-sought-for waterway.

In 1672 the French governor, who was soon to be replaced,

decided before he left for France to make one last try for the glory of finding the Mississippi. He had already sent out two explorers who had not yet returned. One of them had a younger brother, and this brother, Louis Jolliet, seemed the next best person to send. Young Jolliet had already gone as far west as the entrance to Lake Superior, where his family had a large fur trading post. Also, the governor knew that Louis was an expert in the art of drawing maps. This he had learned as a schoolboy from the Jesuit fathers in Quebec. They still treasured a map of the St. Lawrence River that Louis made when he was thirteen. Naturally he was delighted to have been chosen for the expedition and hastened to share the joyful news with the head of the Jesuits in Quebec.

And how happy he himself would be, said the good father, to go along as missionary to the Indians! Since that was impossible, why did not Louis take his friend Père Marquette—a dear, good man, who spoke six Indian languages and was then at the mission at the upper end of Lake Michigan. Louis agreed that it would be a pleasure to have the company of Father Marquette.

According to his arrangement with the governor, Jolliet was to furnish two canoes and all the equipment for the expedition in exchange for the fur trading rights. Five men were quite willing to go along for their share of the furs. They left in October, three men in each canoe with food for the winter, hatchets, knives, beads and cloth for trading with the Indians.

Montreal was the starting point. From there they traveled along two rivers into Lake Huron and on west to the Jolliet trading post to wait through the winter. The bitter cold seemed endless. But at last the ice began cracking and by May it had melted enough to launch the canoes and continue the journey.

Père Marquette, who had received his invitation, was ready and waiting to be picked up at the mission. His portable altar and candles were soon packed in beside Jolliet's precious compass and map-making tools. After kneeling in prayer, the seven men started down the shore of Lake Michigan, heading for Green Bay. From there they followed a small river which brought them to an Indian village, where the chief supplied two guides to lead them to the next river they had been told to follow.

The Indians called it the Wisconsin. Left alone on the strange river, the Frenchmen followed it for six days, wondering if, as the Indians said, it really did empty into the Mississippi. On the seventh foggy morning, still in doubt, they rounded a wooded island and there, stretching before them so wide as to be unmistakable, was the river they had come to find—the great Mississippi!

For a week they traveled south on its smooth surface, seeing no sign of human life, hearing almost no sound but that of their paddles moving through the water. Then suddenly, Père Marquette pointed to the west bank where he saw a path. Could that path, he wondered, lead to the village of Illinois Indians he had been hoping to find? The Indians had been driven from their home across the river by a hostile tribe of Iroquois and had sent a messenger to the good father asking him to visit them.

Though they took the risk of being captured or killed, Marquette and Jolliet followed the narrow path. Fortunately it led them to the village of the Illinois, where they were given a warm welcome. As they were leaving the chief thanked them for coming and presented each one with a parting gift. For Père Marquette he had a beautiful peace pipe of polished gray stone.

"Take with thee this calumet," he said. "It will be honored by every tribe as a sign of brotherhood."

Next, motioning to a small nine-year-old boy to come to him, he said to Jolliet, "Here is my son, whom I give thee to show my heart."

Jolliet could not bear to take the little Indian, but his father insisted. And later, though he looked utterly miserable, the small brave did not shed a tear as he sat in the canoe, watching his homeland disappear.

The Frenchmen had not gone many miles farther down the Mississippi when, rushing into it from the west with a dreadful tumult and roar, came a huge, swirling, muddy river —the Missouri—carrying with it whole trees torn up by the roots and covered with jagged branches. It took fast, skillful paddling before the Frenchmen in their delicate birchbark canoes were out of danger.

They had passed the beautiful green Ohio and had almost reached the mouth of the Arkansas, when suddenly they were in danger again. Yells and war whoops came from the shore. Arrows spattered around them, followed by rocks and stones. Young braves in heavy dugout canoes surrounded them and

CALUMET

with yells of triumph towed them ashore. Père Marquette kept holding up his peace pipe. Finally an old Indian on the shore saw it and cried out to the young warriors, who were then forced to release their captives and treat them as friends.

Jolliet had long since discarded the idea that the Great River led to China, but no Indian, young or old, in that Arkansas village, could say where it did go or how far it was to the sea. In a nearby village, however, the elders of the tribe said it was ten days journey to the mouth of the river. They never went there themselves, but they traded with a tribe who did and from them had received these fine knives and hatchets. Jolliet's heart sank, for he could see that the knives and hatchets had been made in Spain. What he suspected must be true. The Mississippi was the same river which a Spanish explorer had discovered over a hundred years ago and had claimed for Spain!

They would have to turn back. It would be foolhardy for seven unarmed Frenchmen to invade territory claimed by Spain. So there at the mouth of the Arkansas the journey of Marquette and Jolliet ended. Eight years later another French explorer, with forty armed men, would reach the end of the river. His name was La Salle.

La Salle   Frontenac

LA SALLE'S FULL NAME was Robert Cavelier, Sieur de La Salle. He was born in France and in 1666, when he was twenty-three, he came to New France to seek his fortune. Three years later he started out for China, hopefully, by way of the Ohio River! By the time he had returned from exploring the Ohio, the new governor had arrived from France: the Count de Frontenac, an elegant nobleman old enough to be La Salle's father.

The old nobleman and the young explorer liked each other immediately and were drawn together by the same desire to grow rich. Frontenac had lost his inherited fortune and was hoping to gain another in the fur trade. His idea was to build a fort at the head of Lake Ontario where the French could get furs from the Indians before the Indians had a chance to sell them to the English. La Salle thought this was a great idea and helped establish the fort. Frontenac was so impressed by everything that La Salle said and did that he sent him to the court of France with letters of high praise.

The king, Louis XIV, rewarded La Salle for his services by making him a nobleman and granting him a huge estate including the new Fort Frontenac. La Salle returned to New France, enlarged the fort and began making a fine profit in the fur trade for himself and Frontenac.

But what, he said to the governor, was one single fort? Only a beginning. What he, La Salle, planned to do was to build a whole string of forts along the Ohio and on down the Mississippi. All he needed for the venture was permission from the king. So back he went to France where he was again successful. He returned with the right to explore the west and build forts where they were needed—but at his own expense.

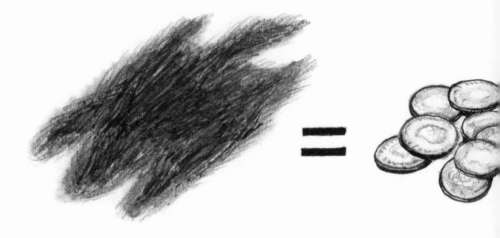

That was no problem for La Salle. He quickly persuaded many men to loan him the money in exchange for their share of the furs he would be sending back. Full of self-confidence, La Salle set forth with nineteen men on what was to be his great fort-building expedition. It turned out to be one long story of disaster, which began even before the first fort was built. This fort was to be at the end of Lake Ontario just above Niagara Falls.

The small ship on which La Salle sailed to Niagara from Fort Frontenac, and which was to be used for the rest of the trip, was battered to pieces in a storm while still anchored in Lake Ontario. So besides building the fort, the explorers had to build a new ship.

a *Griffin*

By spring the ship was finished. They named it *The Griffin* after the mythical animal on Count Frontenac's coat of arms, and that summer La Salle and his nineteen men sailed *The Griffin* to Green Bay. From there he had a small crew take it back loaded with furs to Fort Niagara to repay some of the money he had borrowed. It was to be brought back as soon as possible to the south end of Lake Michigan, where La Salle and the others would be waiting. *The Griffin* was never seen again.

After weeks of waiting for it, La Salle led his disgruntled

men on foot around the end of Lake Michigan into the land of the Illinois Indians. There, in January 1680, they built another fort on the Illinois River and started to build another ship, but soon found they needed more tools and equipment. Though it was March, the worst time of the year to travel, La Salle was determined to go back to Fort Frontenac and get what was needed. With four Frenchmen and one Indian hunter in two canoes, he set out on a horrible journey. Since the Illinois River was still frozen, they began by chopping ice and paddling through the floating ice cakes. Later they discarded the canoes and went on foot, at times plodding through marshes in mud and icy water up to their waists. At night, they slept rolled in blankets on top of logs or piles of branches. Not daring to build a fire for fear of being seen by hostile Indians, their clothes were frozen stiff by morning. On Easter Sunday, gaunt and half starved, they reached Fort Niagara. There La Salle learned that *The Griffin* had never arrived with the furs. His creditors had never been paid. Later he learned that the Illinois fort had been completely destroyed. So the whole expedition was a complete failure. But La Salle did not accept failure. He would try again.

By fall, La Salle had managed to borrow more money and

NORTH AMERICA

UNEXPLORED

FRANCE

ENGLAND

SPAIN

LAND
CLAIMED BY
EUROPEANS

ALGONQUINS

HURONS

IROQUOIS

NEZ
PERCÉS

SIOUX

ALGONQUINS

ILLINOIS

DELAWARES

POWHATAN

CHEROKEES

NAVAHOS

PUEBLOS

CREEKS

SEMINOLES

AZTECS

HOMELAND
OF THE
INDIANS

was on his way west again through the Great Lakes to the south end of Lake Michigan. There he selected forty armed men for the rest of the journey down the Mississippi—twenty-three Frenchmen and seventeen Indians. And this time, instead of trying to build a ship, they went in canoes. By January of the new year, they were paddling down the Illinois River. By February, they had reached the Mississippi and were moving swiftly along. By March, they had passed the mouth of the Arkansas, where Marquette and Jolliet had turned back. Entering the steamy bayous to the south, they saw no sign of Spaniards or of hostile Indians and a month later were at the end of their long journey.

They stood on a point of land looking out upon the Gulf of Mexico. As a record they set up a stone on which they had carved the date and the name of the king of France. Then, while the soldiers stood at attention and the Indians watched in silence, La Salle made this proclamation:

"In the name of the most high, mighty and invincible victorious Prince, Louis the Great, Fourteenth of that name, I, this ninth day of April, one thousand six hundred eighty-two, do now in the name of his Majesty, take possession of this country—Louisiana."

PART THREE

introducing
LOUIS XIV

The Famous "Sun King"

for whom Louisiana was named and who was

KING OF FRANCE

for seventy-two years

1643–1715

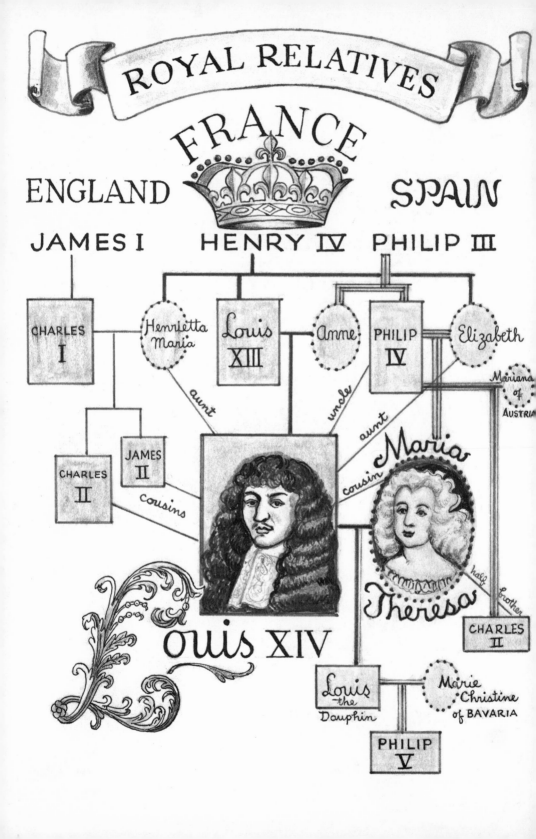

THIS FAT-FACED LITTLE BOY is Louis XIV as he looked when he became king, which was in 1643, the year before William Penn was born. Louis was not quite five, so his mother was put in charge of the government. Since this was far too much for her to manage alone, she invited Cardinal Mazarin, a young Italian churchman of whom she was very fond, to be her prime minister.

So Cardinal Mazarin became the actual ruler of France. Little Louis, meanwhile, played with his toy soldiers and learned to read and write.

74

He was also learning what it meant to be a king, by carefully copying in his penmanship book such sentences as this:

Homage is due to kings. Kings do as they please.

Louis liked Cardinal Mazarin and obediently did and said whatever the cardinal told him to. Not until he was almost ten did he realize that everyone in Paris did not feel as he did about his good friend the cardinal. One day to his great surprise he heard angry crowds in the street below the palace windows shouting and screaming, "Down with Mazarin," and blaming him for the awful taxes they had to pay. Soon after that, something happened that Louis was never to forget.

One dark night he was wakened out of a sound sleep to see his mother bending over him. Carrying a small flickering lantern, she hurried him down a tiny secret stairway into the palace courtyard. There a coach was waiting in which they escaped to another palace outside Paris where Louis would be safe until the war was over.

A civil war had begun that was to last four years. It had been started by members of Parliament who were determined to limit the power of Mazarin. Before the war was over all kinds of angry, jealous, discontented people were mixed up in it, even princes and noblemen. Fortunately for Mazarin,

75

these various groups were not united under a strong leader. So they had to make peace at last without having limited his power in the least.

As for the young king, he was still hailed and adored as the Lord's anointed at his coronation ceremony, which took place after the war. Louis, who was then fifteen, was well aware of his good fortune. He knew that in England, after a similar war against Parliament, the king had been beheaded. The king's son, Charles II, who was Louis's cousin, was then in France. A penniless exile, he was to be drifting about Europe for the next eight years, until he received the joyful invitation to return home.

In 1660, the same year that Charles II went home to become England's Merry Monarch, Louis XIV obediently married his Spanish cousin, Maria Theresa, the bride picked out for him by Cardinal Mazarin.

1661

And now in the life of this most obedient young king, we have reached a year so full of surprises that it came to be known as "Annus Mirabilis," Latin words meaning marvelous, miraculous, almost incredible year.

THE FIRST SURPRISE OF THAT YEAR followed the death of Cardinal Mazarin, which came on the ninth of March, between two and three o'clock in the morning. Louis burst into tears when he was told of it.

"Then suddenly," he said, "I felt for the first time that I was truly the king."

This feeling, in turn, made him brave enough to follow

77

the last advice given him by the cardinal, when later that morning, he held his first council meeting.

The members came expecting to hear which one of them was to be the new prime minister. Those who had been thinking that Louis was so obedient because he had no mind of his own were in for a great surprise.

"Gentlemen," he said, "I have summoned you to tell you that in the future I shall be my own prime minister. You shall all report directly to me."

That had been the cardinal's first piece of advice. "Take the government into your own hands," he had said, well aware of Louis's natural ability. To assist him, the cardinal had recommended a very capable and completely honest man whose name was Colbert.

At the same time he warned Louis against the minister of finance, who had grown immensely rich by stealing from the treasury and snarling up the accounts so he wouldn't be caught. Louis lost no time in appointing Colbert to check on the dishonest minister. Gradually, through very careful figuring, he was caught, condemned and sentenced by the king to life imprisonment.

"I'm glad," said Louis, "to have people see I'm no such

dupe as they thought I was." He was speaking to his mother, who was both surprised and pleased to see her son spending eight hours a day working with Colbert.

Most of the council members thought that being his own prime minister was just a passing fad with the king and would not last long. He was too fond of all kinds of amusements, too busy staging plays, ballets, balls and operas at one of his country palaces, as well as riding and hunting with his friends.

And also making love to his newest sweetheart, a blonde blue-eyed girl named Louise La Vallière. Most people did not expect him to be faithful to the Spanish wife who had been chosen for the good of the state.

Poor Maria Theresa. She was so dumpy and dull and tearful, though she was a little happier when she became the mother of a baby boy.

To celebrate the birth of his son and heir, Louis staged a medieval jousting match in an open space in front of the palace. He wore a costume of orange-red and carried a shield on which was painted a golden sun. The other knights carried shields showing various planets that revolve around the sun. It so pleased Louis to see himself as the center of his world,

that he soon made the sun his official symbol and was known as the SUN KING.

Louis continued to work as hard as he played, never seeming to run out of energy—fortunately, for there was much to be done. France was the largest nation in Europe, having over twice as many people as either England or Spain. But after many years of war France was bankrupt. The treasury was empty; many people were starving. That was the sad fact to which Louis now turned his attention.

"Everyone in my kingdom," he said, "shall have enough to eat, either by working for it or by state help."

But how, when the national treasury was empty and there

were not even enough factories to give everyone work?

Colbert solved that problem by inducing expert workmen from other countries to come to France and establish factories. Cloth makers and weavers came from Belgium; metal workers from Germany; lace makers and glass blowers from Italy; leather workers from Spain; steel workers from England; sugar refiners from Holland.

Colbert was a genius, as hard-working as he was brilliant. In ten years, with his help, Louis XIV brought his impoverished country back to prosperity. Then in 1672, he began to tear it down again, first by going to war against the smallest but richest country in Europe, which was Holland. And second, by building for himself the most elaborate and expensive palace in the entire world—the palace of Versailles.

From then on, he thought only of his own glory. He no longer cared about relieving the peasants, who had been taxed until they were starving to death. He even blamed Colbert, who had served him so faithfully, for not being able to raise money as fast as Louis was spending it. In 1682, the year before Colbert died, sick at heart and discouraged, Louis XIV, disregarding his advice, moved the seat of government from Paris to Versailles.

Versailles

VERSAILLES WAS NOT YET FINISHED, though work had been going on for ten years. There were still 36,000 men and 6,000 horses at work, mainly in the gardens, which covered 230 acres, all laid out in formal patterns, as you see on the map. There were large pools, small lakes and 1,400 fountains. Reflected in the pools and standing among the trees were marble statues of Apollo, Zeus, Neptune, Venus and all

82

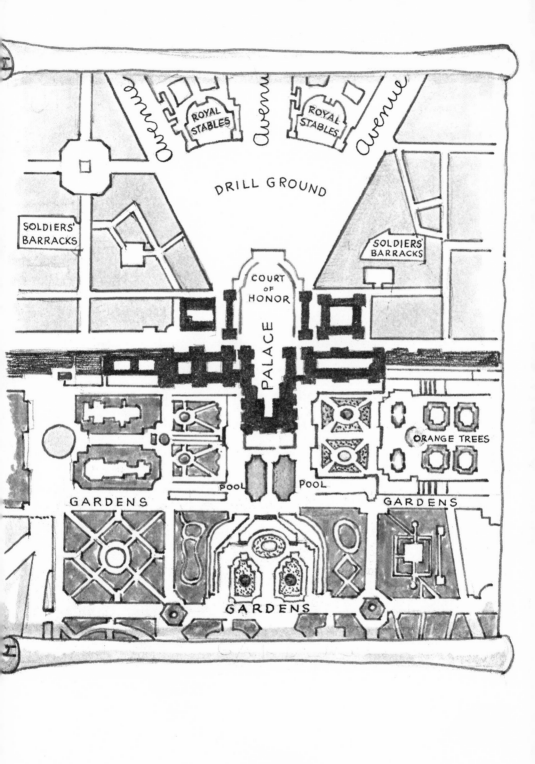

the other gods and goddesses of ancient Greece. In one year alone over 25,000 large trees were hauled there from forests over a hundred miles away. A thousand orange trees in tubs were brought from the former mansion of the minister of finance, who was then in prison.

Originally, Versailles had been a royal hunting lodge where Louis had often gone with his young friends and his first sweetheart, Louise. It was not large enough so he engaged an architect named Mansart to turn it into a palace. In 1682, Mansart was just finishing the magnificent Hall of Mirrors.

This was a vast reception hall in the center of the palace. It had seventeen high round-topped windows looking out on the garden, and on the opposite wall seventeen mirrors the same size and shape. The ceiling was covered with paintings by an artist named Le Brun, showing glorious events in the life of Louis XIV.

Behind the Hall of Mirrors facing the courtyard was the king's apartment. The south wing was for the queen and royal princes. The north wing was for the nobles. The wings were so huge that people hired sedan chairs like taxis to carry them about.

During the day, the Hall of Mirrors was very much like a

street, there was so much traffic with five thousand people living under one roof.

All the nobles and courtiers were obliged to live with the king at Versailles. No one could leave without his permission. Occasionally they were allowed to visit their country estates, but never to go to Paris. He was taking no chance of having them get their heads together and start another civil war. When the king himself went to war against one of the neighboring countries, they went with him. But fighting continued only during spring and summer; the rest of the year the courtiers were at Versailles. To keep them amused and busy Louis arranged all kinds of entertainments, in which they revolved around him from morning to night like planets around the sun. His daily life was a public performance they were expected to attend.

Every day as soon as the king was awake, had washed his hands in wine and chose his wig for the day, one hundred or so courtiers filed in to watch him dress. One by one, those who had the privilege handed him his ruffled shirt, knee breeches, silk stockings, shoes with red heels and diamond buckles, lace handkerchief, gloves, cane, sword and fine red feathered hat.

He then went to his study, where he issued orders for the day and conferred with ambassadors.

Then he went to mass in the palace chapel. After mass he conferred with his council.

Then came the noon meal, carried on silver platters from the kitchens by ten servants.

If a courtier happened to meet the procession, he had to remove his hat, make a low bow, saying reverently, "the king's meat."

The king dined alone, as the courtiers watched, each hoping to be spoken to or, as a special honor, invited to go stag hunting in the afternoon. Violins were always playing while he ate. And on his walks in the garden he was accompanied by musicians playing flutes, oboes and trombones. Toward evening he spent another hour or more in his study. At ten o'clock came his main meal, which he also ate alone, in front of the usual audience. He often ate a tremendous dinner, consisting of four platefuls of soup, a whole pheasant, a partridge, a plate of salad, a portion of mutton, two slices of ham, and finished off with pastries, fruits and sweets for dessert. After this came a ball, concert, card games, billiards, or best of all, a comedy by Molière.

MOLIERE, LIKE SHAKESPEARE, who died just six years
before Molière was born, was both an actor and a playwright.
He was one of a traveling troupe of players who came to Paris
to perform for Louis XIV and his court shortly before the king
was married. They played a tragic drama by Corneille. After

the last curtain, Molière, who had played the leading part, came out and thanked His Majesty for allowing them to appear before him, and then humbly begged his permission to present a small play of his own. It was a comedy about a doctor which did not please the courtiers at all but utterly delighted Louis XIV. He saw at once that Molière was a genius, had his troupe settle in Paris and gave them the use of the theater in the Palais Royal.

Four days after Louis XIV and his new bride Maria Theresa arrived from Spain, they went to see a comedy by Molière in which he poked fun at some of the foolish, affected mannerisms of the day. Louis often had a suggestion for Molière. One of these became a play called "The Would-be Gentleman," which was about a plain man who made himself ridiculous by aping the fine manners of a courtier. Molière's last play, "The Imaginary Invalid," was about one of those people who always imagine they are sick. Strangely enough Molière died while he was playing the part. That was the year 1673.

That year Louis XIV was not in Paris. He was on the battlefield in Holland, playing his favorite role of Louis le Grand, the glorious warrior.

THE WAR AGAINST HOLLAND was the second of four
wars which Louis XIV started in Europe to increase the size
and importance of France and to win glory for himself. One
look at the map convinced him that the Rhine River ought
to be his northeastern border line. To make it so meant taking
four pieces of land, one each from Holland and Germany, and

two from Spain, the Franche-Comté and the Spanish Nether-lands. War against Spain came first.

In 1665, Maria Theresa's father, King Philip, died. Since her dowry had never been paid, Louis XIV claimed that the Spanish Netherlands belonged to her. The new king of Spain naturally objected and war began. England, Sweden and Holland rushed to the aid of Spain. So all that Louis could take from the Spanish Netherlands were a few towns along the border. War with Holland came next.

On a soft April day in Paris, Louis XIV bade farewell to his newest lady love, Madame de Montespan, donned his wide hat with its waving red plumes and rode off to war in command of 100,000 well-trained troops in handsome uniforms. In less than six weeks the French troops had crossed the Rhine and were within sight of the city of Amsterdam. At this time Holland, less than one-sixteenth of the size of France, was the wealthiest nation in Europe. It had the largest navy in the world and the richest bank, the Bank of Amsterdam. Louis's eyes shone with the thought that all of these riches would soon be his. He counted on his conquest too soon.

That year, 1672, William III, Prince of Orange, a small, slight but most determined and very capable young Dutch-

WILLIAM OF ORANGE

man, was made stadtholder of the United Netherlands and put in charge of the war against France.

Amsterdam and most of Holland lie below sea level. When William realized that it was impossible to stop the French army in any other way, he had the dykes cut and let the waters of the sea rush in, forcing the French soldiers to either retreat or be drowned.

Spain and Germany then came to the aid of Holland. The

war went on for six years until both sides were exhausted and ready to stop and make peace. Although Louis XIV got nothing from Holland, he managed by very skillful manoeuvering to acquire thirty-four more cities in the Spanish Netherlands. And also the Franche-Comté.

He returned to Paris in triumph. There two arches were erected in his honor, like those built to honor the conquering Caesars returning to ancient Rome. The title of "Le Grand Monarch" was also accorded him. He was Louis the Great, the most absolute, the most powerful monarch in Europe. He had reached the peak of his glory, but he still envied the wealth of little Holland.

Most of Holland's immense wealth came from her rich trade with the Far East, especially with the East Indies. Before Louis XIV's war with Holland was over, Colbert, always pressed for money, had formed a French East India Trading Company and established a French trading post on the southeast coast of India.

Long before that, England, also eager to compete with the Dutch, had formed an East India Trading Company and established several trading posts in India, for which both English and French paid an annual rent to the Mogul emperors.

PART FOUR

introducing

Two Mogul Emperors of India

SHAH JAHAN

who built the beautiful

TAJ MAHAL

and his warrior son

AURANGZEB ALAMGIR

the last of the Great Moguls

who ruled from

1658 to 1707

Shah Jahan

ONE OF THE MOST BEAUTIFUL BUILDINGS in the
world is the lovely Taj Mahal, which was being built in India
while Louis XIV was a small boy. It is not a palace nor a
church, but a tomb. The tomb of Mumtaz Mahal, the favorite
wife of the great Mogul emperor Shah Jahan, who then ruled
over northern India.

Shah Jahan was heartbroken when his beloved one died
and planned for her a tomb as "beautiful as she was." It was

95

to be of white marble, inlaid with jewels and decorated with lacework of stone. To turn his dream into reality, he summoned expert craftsmen from all over India and Asia, and even some from Italy, to his capital city of Agra. They worked for twenty-two years.

He also founded the city of Delhi, which is the modern capital of India. Part of the city is still called Shah-jahan-abad, the city of Shah Jahan.

Across the river from the Taj Mahal, the emperor had hoped to build for himself a tomb of black marble and have the two tombs connected by a silver bridge. It was never built. Shah Jahan spent the last eight years of his life imprisoned in the fort at Agra. He was put there by one of his sons, who had rebelled against him, seized the throne and made himself emperor.

Shah Jahan died in 1666, which happened to be the year of the great fire of London, when the English architect Christopher Wren began rebuilding the city of London.

The Shah's coffin was placed beside that of his beloved wife in the Taj Mahal. There they are today side by side beneath the central dome of that beautiful tomb which keeps alive the memory of their love.

96

AURANGZEB WAS THE NAME OF THE SON who imprisoned his father, had his three brothers murdered and declared himself emperor. Unlike his father, who was a poet and an artist, this son cared for only two things, war and religion, the Moslem religion. This religion had been brought to India by his Mongol ancestor, who had come down from

The MOGUL EMPIRES of INDIA

EMPIRE OF SHAH JAHAN

Delhi
Agra
THE GANGES RIVER
Calcutta

EMPIRE
CONQUERED
BY
AURANGZEB

unconquered

AURANGZEB

ALAMGIR

Asia, conquered the Hindu princes of northern India and founded the Mogul (or Mongol) dynasty.

Aurangzeb was not satisfied with the empire of his ancestors. His ambition was to conquer all of the Hindu princes, suppress the Hindu religion and make all of India into a Moslem state.

Aurangzeb was as fearless as he was ambitious. Once, when he was fifteen, he had shown such courage against a fighting elephant that his father rewarded him with a sword. On it was engraved the word "Alamgir," meaning "Conqueror of the World." So when he became emperor, Aurangzeb took the title of AURANGZEB ALAMGIR.

In 1681 (the year that William Penn received his Charter from Charles II) Aurangzeb set out from Delhi to conquer southern India and never came back. The remaining twenty-six years of his life were spent in camp, on the march or on the battlefield. In battle he rode on top of a huge elephant, which was covered with heavy armor. Sometimes he had the elephant's feet chained to the ground so that it could not turn and run in the midst of the fight. In the end, Aurangzeb conquered all of India, except the very tip. But in doing that, he conquered more territory than he, or anyone of the Mogul emperors who followed him, was able to control. So began the downfall of the Mogul empire.

Not very long after Aurangzeb had started out from Delhi, he heard that war had broken out between his officials and the English traders at one of the English trading posts. He immediately issued a decree that all English trading posts be seized and all trade with the English stopped. However, he soon discovered that when the trade stopped, so too did the rents and the profits and the taxes from the goods that were sold. After four years, Aurangzeb issued a new decree, saying that since "the English have made a most humble petition and will present the emperor with a fine of 150,000 rupees and behave no more in so shameful a manner, his Majesty hath pardoned their faults and agrees that they follow their trade as in former times."

Six months later the English founded the city of Calcutta at the mouth of the Ganges River, which later was to be their capital when they, instead of the Moguls, ruled over India.

In 1757, exactly fifty years after Aurangzeb died, England gained control of India and held it until 1947. Then at last, after 400 years of being under the rule of foreigners, India regained its independence.

PART FIVE

introducing

SIR ISAAC NEWTON

who discovered the Laws of Gravity

EDMUND HALLEY

who studied comets

and other scientists whose work

made the years of William Penn

THE GREAT AGE

OF SCIENCE

Isaac Newton

December 25, 1642

ON CHRISTMAS DAY, 1642, when Isaac Newton was born, no one thought he would live to grow up. He weighed only three pounds and was so tiny his mother declared, "You could have put him into a quart mug." His father never saw him; he had died before the baby was born.

By the time Isaac was seven he had begun reading, writing and arithmetic in a small school in the town of Woolsthorpe, Lincolnshire, which was his birthplace. At twelve he was sent to the King's School at Grantham, about six miles away, where he boarded with the town druggist. All the money his mother sent him Isaac spent on tools, and all the time he should have spent on his lessons he used up inventing or making some kind of mechanical device. First it was a sundial; then a water clock, which ran by water dripping through a hole (until the hole got clogged up).

Next came the model of a windmill, which he set up on the roof of the druggist's house. Instead of having it run by wind, in the ordinary way, Isaac put a mouse inside and let the mouse do the work. Almost every day curious townsfolk stopped by to see Isaac's "mouse miller." And to feed it, farmers in the market gladly supplied the young inventor with handfuls of corn.

In school, meanwhile, Isaac did so poorly in everything but mathematics that he was taken out after a couple of years and put to work on the home farm. The result was much the same. The sheep he was supposed to be tending wandered away while Isaac was busy whittling models, building dams in the creek or waterwheels in the brook. Often he was so absorbed in what he was doing that he forgot to go in for dinner.

One day he was sent to Grantham on an errand. Coming back he got off his horse to lead it up a very steep hill and then was so busy thinking he forgot to get on again and walked the rest of the way home.

Since it was plain to see that Isaac would never make a farmer, his mother took the advice of the headmaster, sent her son back to school and had him tutored in those studies in which he showed no interest of his own. He excelled in mathematics, and on the day of his graduation the headmaster "spoke with the pride of a father" in praise of young Newton's character and talents.

Isaac then entered the University of Cambridge, where his teacher in geometry saw at once that his new student was a genius. Isaac Newton spent the next four years at Cambridge, and upon graduation he was offered a fellowship to continue his studies. But by that time the awful plague which was killing so many people in London had reached Cambridge, and the University had to be closed. It also remained closed during the next year, in which over half of London was destroyed by fire.

For Isaac Newton those two years, which he spent at home in Woolsthorpe, proved to be the most amazing years of his life as well as two most remarkable years in the history of science.

Robert Boyle

The Royal Society
Robert Boyle
Robert Hooke
Christopher Wren
John Flamsteed
Isaac Newton
Edmund Halley
Samuel Pepys
William Penn

THE YEAR THAT ISAAC NEWTON entered college, the Merry Monarch Charles II was crowned king of England. The new king had already heard about a society in London whose members met to discuss all kinds of natural science.

There was another such society in Oxford, he was told, which met at the lodgings of an Irish chemist, Robert Boyle, who was especially interested in measuring and weighing different kinds of gas.

The king laughed when he heard that scientists were try-

Christian Huygens

ing to weigh air and actually talked of a time when men would be able to fly. Yet he had no doubt that their discussions about astronomy, physics, mechanics and so forth would lead to worthwhile discoveries. What if they should actually succeed in turning lead into gold! Soon Charles II combined the two societies into one, calling it the Royal Society of London.

One of the original members was the architect Sir Christopher Wren. At all the meetings, interesting experiments were performed. The day that Samuel Pepys became a member, he wrote in his diary that they had studied "the nature of fire."

The Royal Society soon began publishing a magazine to print findings from Holland, Italy and France as well as their own. For not only in England, but all over Europe, people were interested in the new learning. Language was no problem, because all scientists and scholars in Europe wrote and spoke Latin.

In France, an Academy of Science was established by Louis XIV. One of the large paintings at Versailles shows the twenty-four original members receiving their charter from the Sun King. Soon after the academy was established Louis had an observatory built in Paris and invited a noted Italian astronomer to become its first director. Scientists from all the various European countries were invited to become members of the French academy and to live and work in Paris. Christian Huygens, a famous scientist from Holland, accepted the invitation, even though his country was at war with France.

"The world is my country," he said, "and to promote science is my religion."

Most scientists felt as he did. Science was above national boundaries. It united rather than divided people of the world.

THE YOUNG UNKNOWN STUDENT, Isaac Newton, had then made the two discoveries about gravity and light that were to make his name famous.

For some time before he left Cambridge he had been

thinking about sunlight, wondering what it was made of. One day at Sturbridge Fair he had seen and bought something he thought would be of use to him. It was a glass prism, which he could hardly wait to try. As soon as he was home in Woolsthorpe, he set up his experiment.

First he closed the shutters in his room, leaving just one small hole through which a single ray of sunlight came streaming in. Holding the prism in the light and turning it this way and that, he soon saw the ray of white light being broken up into various colored rays, each coming out of the prism at a different angle. On the wall the colors always appeared in the same order, red, orange, yellow, green, blue, indigo, violet.

Several years later, based on his experiment, he invented a new kind of telescope, which he presented to the Royal Society. Then, as a new member, he sent them a report entitled, "New Theory about Light and Color."

By then, however, other scientists had been experimenting with light and disagreed with Newton as to the way in which light traveled. In fact, his report caused so much argument and criticism that Newton vowed never again to write about any discovery he might make.

WHAT HELD THE UNIVERSE TOGETHER? That was another question young Isaac Newton had been wondering about. What kept the earth and planets revolving around the sun? What kept the moon continually circling the earth instead of flying off into space?

With any puzzling question, Newton first tried to imagine what the answer might be and then prove it right or wrong by mathematics.

According to an old story, the answer to this question about the universe came to Newton one afternoon as he was having tea in the garden. An apple happened to fall to the ground and started a train of thought.

Why didn't the apple fly off into space? he asked himself. No need to ask anyone such a simple question! The apple was attracted to the center of the earth by a force called gravity. Suddenly, in a flash, Newton saw that the same force which attracted the apple to the earth must also attract the moon to the earth, the earth to the sun and the planets to one another. That was it! The entire universe was held together by gravity!

To prove it by mathematics, he took the size of the earth, the size of the moon and its distance from the earth, compared to the size and distance of the apple.

After careful figuring, he was disappointed. Unable to find his mistake, he sadly laid the figures away.

The next year, 1667, he was back at Cambridge. Two years later he replaced his mathematics teacher, who had recommended him as an "unparalleled genius," which he was in mathematics. As a teacher he was a dismal failure.

"So few students went to hear him," his secretary said,

"that sometimes there was no one there at all and he returned sadly to his rooms."

Working in his laboratory, he would soon forget everything outside. He hardly ever went to the dining hall. When he did it was plain to see he had not combed his hair nor pulled up his wrinkled stockings.

For twelve years Newton went on living his quiet life at Cambridge, until one day he heard news from France that sent him trembling with excitement to find the figures on gravity he had laid away so long ago.

At the Paris Observatory, a French astronomer had discovered that the earth was larger than it was generally supposed to be. There were 360 degrees of longitude around the earth. But each degree, the Frenchman said, was about 69 miles wide instead of about 60.

Those extra 9 miles, thought Newton, 9 times 360! Those new figures would give him the right answer. Now he could prove his theory about universal gravity!

Once that was done, he laid the figures away again. He was satisfied. He felt no need to talk to anyone about his discovery. Certainly he would send no announcement of it to the Royal Society!

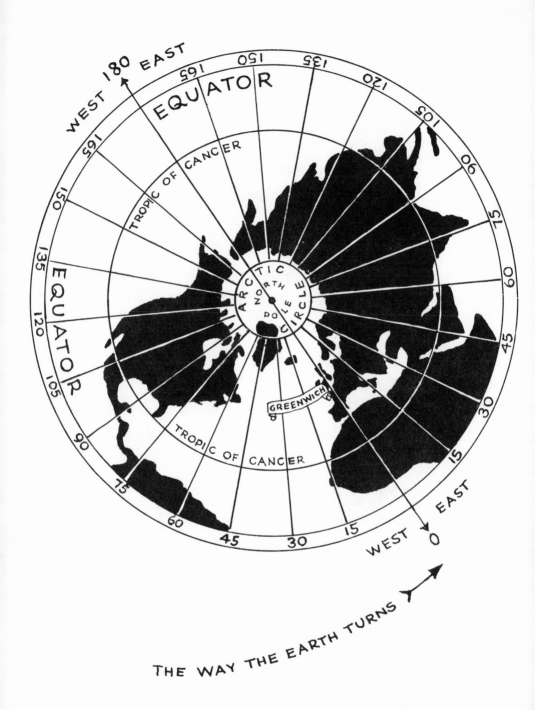

THE WAY THE EARTH TURNS

THE PARIS OBSERVATORY had been founded mainly because astronomy was necessary for navigation. Ships at sea found their way by means of the stars. The English had a larger navy than the French but it was not until later that Charles II founded the Royal Observatory at Greenwich southeast of London.

The building was designed by Sir Christopher Wren. On its roof was a "time ball," which the chief astronomer dropped each day at 1 P.M. to signal the correct time in England according to the sun.

Today the signal is sent by radio. And not only in England, but everywhere around the world, clocks are set according to the time at Greenwich.

There are twenty-four time zones around the world (one for each hour of the day); each one is fifteen degrees of longitude wide. Going east from Greenwich each zone is from one to twelve hours later than the hour at Greenwich and one to twelve hours earlier going west. So when the sun shines directly down upon Greenwich it is high noon in England, but only six o'clock in the morning in the eastern part of the United States and three hours earlier than that on the Pacific coast.

THE YEAR THE OBSERVATORY AT GREENWICH was founded, Edmund Halley, a student at Oxford, was so eager to become an astronomer that he persuaded his father to let him leave college, go to the South Seas and study the stars. He had heard that the director of the new observatory was making a chart of stars in the northern sky. He would make a similar chart of the southern sky.

King Charles procured passage for him on a trading ship bound for India, and he took off in high spirits for the island of St. Helena, the southernmost island owned by England. There he set up his telescope, charted 341 stars and brought back to London a map of the southern sky as a present for the king. He promptly became one of the youngest and most popular members of the Royal Society.

Another new member was William Penn, who was elected just before he went to Pennsylvania. From there he sent back samples of ore and medicinal herbs to the Irish chemist, Robert Boyle, whom he had known at Oxford.

One afternoon, about the time William Penn returned from America, Edmund Halley and a couple of other members were having a discussion about planets.

What force could it be that kept the planets revolving around the sun, they were asking. How did it vary with the planet's size and distance from the sun?

Since no one in London could answer that question, Halley set out at once for Cambridge to consult another member of the society about it—Mr. Isaac Newton.

"I've already solved that problem," Newton told his astonished guest. He'd forgotten, however, just where the figures were, but they must be somewhere about.

Edmund Halley was so genuinely excited that he was able to persuade the shy, reluctant Newton to send the figures to him later and let them be published by the Royal Society. Unfortunately the society, of which Mr. Samuel Pepys was now the president, did not have money enough to do it.

Very well, said Edmund Halley, he would pay for it himself. Laying aside his own work, he spent two years preparing for the printer what Newton sent and urging him to write more and more about his discoveries. So the world is indebted to Edmund Halley for one of the greatest books on science ever written, Isaac Newton's *Principia*. Published in 1687, its full title in Latin was

PHILOSOPHIAE NATURALIS PRINCIPIA MATHEMATICA
or, reversing the order of the words,
MATHEMATICAL PRINCIPLES OF NATURAL PHILOSOPHY.

IF ON SOME NIGHT IN THE YEAR 1986 you see a comet shining in the sky, you will remember Edmund Halley, for it will be Halley's Comet.

In ancient times when a comet was seen flashing its flaming tail across the sky, it was taken as a sign that the gods were angry and disaster would follow. In the 1600s many people still believed comets were an evil omen.

Edmund Halley's interest in them had begun before his

visit to Isaac Newton in Cambridge. He had seen two comets before that. One was in 1680 at the Paris Observatory, where he had spent several months with the Italian director, and another, two years later.

He was glad to hear Newton say that he also believed comets were regular members of the solar system. Like the planets they too traveled around the sun. But their orbits were so vast that it took many years for them to complete the round trip and be seen again.

After Halley had finished publishing Newton's book, he turned his attention back to the history of comets. He was able to tabulate the paths of twenty-four bright comets that had appeared in the last 300 years. Very soon he noticed that the tracks made in 1456, 1531, 1607 and 1682 were so much alike that they must have been made by the same comet, returning about every seventy-five years. Therefore, though he would not live to see it, Halley predicted that the comet would reappear in 1758. On Christmas Day, 1758, the comet was seen again and given his name by friends who remembered his prophecy. Halley's Comet has appeared regularly on schedule ever since. Its last appearance was in 1910. It will be passing by again in 1986.

ONE DAY THE ROYAL SOCIETY received a lengthy, curious letter written in Dutch from a shopkeeper in Holland who signed himself:

ANTON VAN LEEUWENHOEK

The members had it translated and were amused, first of all, then amazed and astounded by what this man reported having seen through a microscope he had made himself. No wonder they were amazed, for Leeuwenhoek had seen what no one had ever seen before or even knew existed.

From the beginning of time, men had looked up at the sun,

the moon and the stars and wondered what they were. They had seen large animals and had imagined that somewhere much huger monsters, even fire-spitting dragons, might exist. But never had they dreamed that there could be creatures so small as the "wee beasties" that Leeuwenhoek said he had seen in a drop of rain water. Some of these beasties he had measured were a thousand times smaller than the eye of a louse. A million of them could stand on a grain of sand.

To test the truth of this incredible information, the Royal Society appointed two members to build the best possible microscope and make their own observations. They gave their report, and Anton van Leeuwenhoek was promptly made a member of the Royal Society.

And so in that age of science, a whole new world had been discovered, alive with thousands of tiny plants and animals, some deadly to mankind, some friendly and useful—the microscopic world of germs and bacteria.

PART SIX

continuing the life story of
WILLIAM PENN
1684–1699

telling of the disasters that befell him

for being a friend of
KING JAMES II
and why Pennsylvania was taken from him by
WILLIAM and MARY

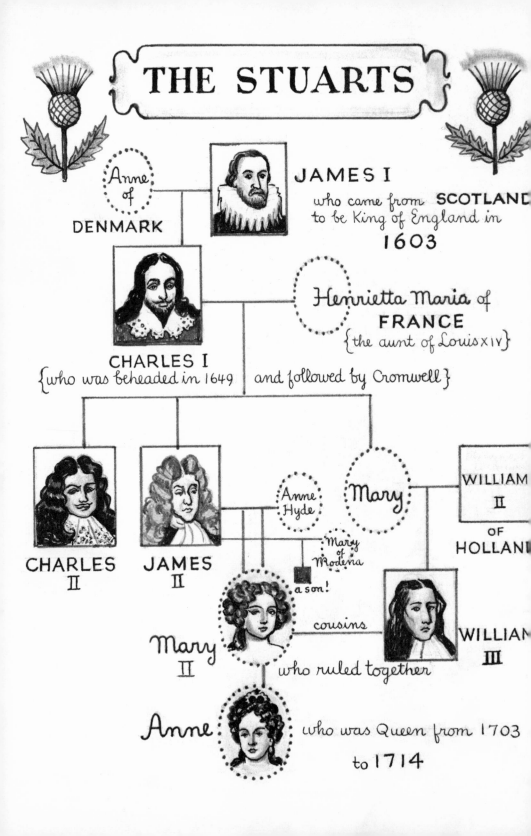

THE STUARTS

Anne of DENMARK

JAMES I
who came from **SCOTLAND**
to be King of England in
1603

CHARLES I
{who was beheaded in 1649   and followed by Cromwell}

Henrietta Maria of **FRANCE**
{the aunt of Louis XIV}

CHARLES II

JAMES II

Anne Hyde

Mary of Modena

a son!

Mary

WILLIAM II of **HOLLAND**

Mary II

cousins

WILLIAM III

who ruled together

Anne   who was Queen from **1703**
to **1714**

James II

"I ARRIVED FROM AMERICA on the sixth of October in Sussex within seven miles of my house." So wrote William Penn in 1684 to a friend in Pennsylvania. After a few happy days spent with Guli and the children, he went up to London. There he called upon King Charles II and the duke of York, both of whom, he said, received him "very graciously." The king however was very ill, and four months later he died.

After being king for twenty-five years, England's Merry Monarch was gone. Since Charles II left no legitimate son to inherit the throne, his brother James, the duke of York, became King James II.

Hardly was the coronation ceremony over before James was in serious trouble. Three years later he was fleeing for his life and William Penn was about to be condemned as a criminal for having been his friend.

Their friendship had begun the year of the plague when the law school was closed and Sir William, the commander, had taken his son to sea with him. Young William spent two weeks aboard the warship with James, the duke of York, who was then the admiral of the navy.

Now, twenty years later, James had become the king of England. And as king, James II was also the head of the Church of England. But James was a Roman Catholic. And with the help of his powerful cousin, Louis XIV, James intended to turn England back into a Catholic country. He began by issuing a Declaration of Indulgence which did away with old laws against Roman Catholics and all others who did not belong to the Church of England. Since that included Quakers, a delegation headed by William Penn went to present their thanks to the king. In reply the king expressed his appreciation and then said, "Some of you know, as I am sure you do, Mr. Penn, that I believe all men ought to have the freedom of their consciences." This, he saw, made a good impression.

Pleased with himself, James went boldly ahead and ordered all bishops in the Church of England to read his Declaration of Indulgence aloud to their congregations. Seven bishops refused. James had those seven bishops seized, arrested and imprisoned in the Tower of London.

In great alarm, William Penn rushed to the king and begged him to set the bishops free. But James, too stubborn to listen to any advice, had the bishops brought to trial. This was a fatal mistake. Even though he had the judges well bribed to see that the bishops were condemned, the jury stood firm and refused to bring in the verdict of guilty. The night that the bishops were set free was celebrated throughout London with fireworks and cannon fire, like the news of a great victory.

By that time, however, there was bad news as well as good. A son had been born to James II and his second wife. That changed the whole royal picture. Until then, Mary, James's

127

oldest daughter—a Protestant—had been heir to the throne. Now instead of Mary, this baby, being a son, was his father's heir. And so the hope that had helped the English people to endure James II was gone.

Mary was married to her cousin, William of Orange, stadtholder of the United Netherlands. Almost as soon as James's baby was born, an invitation was sent to William of Orange to come with an army, overthrow his father-in-law and defend Mary's right to the throne. In November, 1688, William landed in England with 14,000 troops.

James II tried to rally a force to resist him, but all his officers deserted him. Even his younger daughter, Anne, supported the cause of her sister, Mary. One dark night James fled in panic from the palace, crossed the river in a small boat and later reached France where his wife and infant son had already taken refuge.

There Louis XIV attempted to reverse the fate of his cowardly cousin. Supplying James with French troops, Louis XIV sent him off to Ireland, told him to collect more troops, and from there invade England, fight his way back to the throne and drive out that miserable, puny, Protestant usurper, William of Orange.

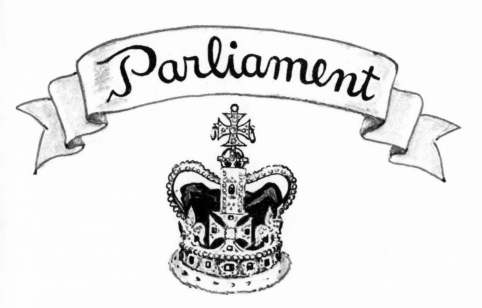

WILLIAM OF ORANGE AND MARY, it was decided, should rule England together as William III and Mary II. Before they left Holland they made a promise "to maintain the liberties of England and the Protestant religion." This promise was lettered on the flag of William's ship. But Parliament was tired of promises made by kings and never kept. So before their coronation William and Mary had to sign a Bill of Rights, so firm that never again could any king overrule the will of the Parliament. This was such a turning point in English history it is known as the "Glorious Revolution."

1688

Shortly after the coronation William III left for Ireland, where he met and defeated James II in a battle in northern Ireland. Ireland was then divided, as it still is, between the Catholics in the south and the Protestants in the north. In the south, where William Penn had his large estate, the Catholics naturally supported James. The Protestants in the north supported William of Orange and from then on were to be called "orange men." The summer after his defeat, James II was safely back in France.

His friend William Penn was a prisoner in the Tower of London, falsely "charged with high treason for abetting and adhering to their Majesties' enemy." He was soon proven innocent in England.

But then in Ireland he was accused of being a traitor and all of his Irish estates were taken from him. It was three years before his name was finally cleared.

Then, when he might have returned to Pennsylvania, Pennsylvania had been taken away from him, because he was a Quaker, and Quakers did not believe in war.

War had broken out between the French and English in America. It was part of the third one of those European wars

started by Louis XIV. This time, to his delight, Louis had
found an excuse to lay claim to the Palatinate, that piece of
German land lying mostly west of the Rhine.

William of Orange promptly formed a league against him,
composed of Holland, two German states, Sweden and Spain.
Three years later, when he became king of England, William
brought England into the war, which then spread to the
American colonies. There it became the first of those colonial
wars that were to last a hundred years until England finally
conquered New France.

The Count de Frontenac, the governor of New France, had started the war in America by sending a posse of Frenchmen and Indians to attack the English settlers in New York. In all the nearby colonies, the settlers stood ready to grab their guns and defend their borders.

All except the Quakers of Pennsylvania. The king of England had therefore reclaimed the colony and placed it under the general in New York. This arrangement had not been working out too well. So the king was quite ready to give Pennsylvania back to William Penn, provided Mr. Penn would promise to contribute money to defend it from the French. The necessary promise was made. And on August 20, 1694, William Penn had his new charter bearing the royal signatures of William III and Mary II.

What then was there to prevent him from returning to America? Nothing except that he had no money, not even enough to pay for the voyage. And he was deep in debt. So another five years were to slip by before William Penn was able to leave for Pennsylvania. And again his beloved Guli would not be with him. She died just six months before the new charter was signed.

PART SEVEN

introducing

K'ANG-HSI

The Great Manchu Emperor

who ruled China for Sixty Years from

1662 to 1722

康熙

K'ANG-HSI, THE MANCHU EMPEROR who ruled China at the time of William Penn, was one of the greatest men ever to rule that ancient land of the friendly dragon. His reign, which was to last for sixty years, began in 1662 when he was eight years old.

It was then in the royal city of Peking that his father, the first Manchu emperor of China, lay dying. It had not been many years since the Manchus had come down from the north and driven out the last of the royal family of Ming, which had been ruling China for almost three hundred years. The nation was still unsettled from the sudden change and the dying emperor was distressed over having to leave the throne to one of his three sons who were all so very young. Of the three, the youngest one was recommended by their teacher as being the brightest and liveliest, so he was chosen by his father. An imperial messenger was sent to the place where he was being brought up, to bring him to the palace to be presented to the court.

The ceremony took place in the hugest hall the small boy had ever seen. It was filled with golden umbrellas, bright, embroidered banners and huge silk fans. They were all about him, high above his head and carried by officials in gorgeous satin robes, who were lined up on either side of the throne—the red dragon throne. Here he himself was seated, dressed in a yellow silk robe, embroidered with golden dragons. As he sat there, with his feet tucked neatly under him in proper fashion, he saw the great lords begin to come forward, one by one, kneel, bow their heads nine times to the ground before him and remain kneeling. Kneeling to him! It seemed unbelievable. Yet he understood why. He was now the emperor, and the emperor was honored as T'ien Tzu, the Son of Heaven. Many times in school he had made the words "Tien Tzu" with his writing brush. Now that most sacred title was his!

Four ministers had been appointed to manage the government until K'ang-hsi himself was old enough to rule. Until then his days were divided between study and play. Hunting and riding were his favorite sports. Soon he could ride and shoot so well that he was able to hit a moving target from the back of a galloping horse.

Since both his father and mother were dead, his Manchu grandmother, a remarkable woman whom K'ang-hsi dearly loved, took charge of his education. The finest scholars were appointed by her to instruct him in all the ancient wisdom of China. Most appealing to the boy were the sayings of Confucius. He especially liked the story of how the master gave his golden rule for living.

It happened that while Confucius was the chief justice of a province, he had tried to settle a quarrel between two herdsmen who could not understand the law. So he gave them one simple rule to follow in the future:

DO NOT DO TO OTHERS WHAT YOU WOULD
NOT HAVE THEM DO TO YOU.

As K'ang-hsi thought about this simple rule, he decided he would try to write some similar rules or maxims that shepherds or peasants or anyone in his empire could understand. At about the same time, he also decided to take control of the government. He was then thirteen. Three years later he had finished writing his maxims. There were sixteen of them, each one exactly seven words long. Many of them, like those of Confucius, were about the respect and honor that children owed their parents both when they were living and after they were dead.

These maxims, known as the Sacred Edict of K'ang-hsi, were read aloud in the law courts twice a month, at the time of the new and the full moon. Year after year this was done, as long as the Manchu dynasty lasted.

That was until 1911, when China ceased to be an empire and became a republic.

138

春
SPRING
夏
SUMMER

秋
AUTUMN
冬
WINTER

THE YEAR 1668 WAS COMING TO AN END. At midnight on December 21, the longest night of the year, when the sun seemed to stand still, the young emperor K'ang-hsi went according to ancient custom to the Temple of Heaven. There on its marble terrace open to the sky, he paid homage to Heaven, whose great Law governed the universe. A few days later, shortly after sunrise, K'ang-hsi sat puzzling over the calendar for 1669 spread before him on his writing ta-

139

ble. Each year the emperor must provide the people with a calendar. But how could he issue a calendar so incorrect as this one? What faith could the people have in a Son of Heaven who seemed not to understand even the simple law governing the seasons?

The astronomer who had prepared the faulty calendar had been appointed by those four ministers who had previously managed the government. He had divided the year as it should be, into days measured by the sun and into months measured by the moon, but he had put the seasons spring, fall, summer, winter all in the wrong months!

Very soon, K'ang-hsi was told that the astronomer from Europe whom he had sent for had arrived. Looking up he saw a large portly bearded man, well past middle age, clad in the coarse black habit of a monk, with sandals on his feet and a cross swinging from his belt.

This was Father Ferdinand Verbiest, a Jesuit priest from Belgium who had come as a missionary to China to teach the Roman Catholic religion.

"I understand from your letter," said K'ang-hsi, "that you are able to make a correct calendar. Can you give me any proof of this?"

F. Verbiest

"Indeed yes," replied Father Verbiest. "If your Majesty will have a straight rod placed upright on a table in full light of the sun, I will draw a line to show where its shadow will fall tomorrow at noon."

Long before noon, mandarins and officials of the court were lined up to see the experiment. Friends of the astronomer who had made the faulty calendar were hoping it would fail. They smiled to see the shadow of the rod so far from the line which the "barbarian priest," as they called him, had drawn on the table. But the shadow moved gradually till at noon, to their amazement, it fell exactly on the line. All, except those jealous few, were full of praise for Father Verbiest.

K'ang-hsi, delighted, made him president of the board of astronomy and provided funds for him to refit the observatory on Peking's eastern wall. Six new instruments were installed, including a sextant, a quadrant and a large globe of the heavens.

K'ang-hsi grew so interested in the observatory that he sent for all the books on astronomy and mathematics that had been written or translated by the Jesuits into Chinese and then sent for Father Verbiest to be his teacher. Learning for K'ang-hsi was a great adventure, discovering new facts, being introduced to new ideas!

He could hardly believe it when he learned that the earth moved around the sun and was not the center of the universe. He was most excited when he was finally able to calculate an eclipse.

An easy natural friendship developed between the young emperor and his teacher, which was most unusual, since everyone, even his nearest relatives, knelt before K'ang-hsi as the Son of Heaven and revered him as a god.

MONGOL 元

K'ANG-HSI'S DAY BEGAN AT SUNRISE, when he met
with his ministers to consider the problems of government.
After that he was free to study, or if the afternoon was fair,
he might go hunting. As there were no lights in the palace,
bedtime came with the dark.

Those peaceful well-ordered days were suddenly cut short
by two wars which broke out at the same time. In the south
a Chinese general had started a rebellion against the Manchu
government, while a Mongol chief and his tribesmen attacked
China's border on the north.

143

The name K'ang-hsi meant "Lasting Peace." That is what the young emperor hoped to establish. He saw no glory in war, nor in being a soldier. He believed what Confucius taught—that there were four classes of people: the soldier was the lowest; the scholar was the highest; and in between were the herdsman and the merchant.

But when it was necessary for him to become a soldier, K'ang-hsi became a good one. He himself commanded the troops that went to restore peace on the northern border.

Before leaving, he visited both the Temple of Heaven and the Temple of his Ancestors, to ask help in the war he was obliged to undertake to restore peace. To prepare his soldiers as they were about to leave, he gave each one of them a cup of wine with his own hands.

Starting out then, he led the troops north beyond the Great Wall, west across the Gobi desert, continually fighting and driving back the Mongols, until the last Mongol stronghold was captured, the last Mongol chieftain had surrendered, and all of Mongolia had become part of the empire of China. By that time the rebellion in the south had also been put down. Pirates who had helped the Chinese rebels were driven from the island of Taiwan, and Taiwan was added to the empire of China. Finally, after eight years of war, the empire was once more at peace, and K'ang-hsi made every effort to keep it so. First he made another journey into Mongolia.

This time he wanted the Mongol chiefs and tribesmen to see him not as an enemy who had defeated them, but as a great and powerful friend who was interested in their welfare. That they should also see him surrounded by all the magnificent splendor of the court, he took the entire court with him, all the mandarins with their servants and retainers. He also took his three favorite wives, each riding in a golden chariot, and his oldest son, who was then ten years old. There were thousands of people, thousands of horses and baggage wagons, thousands of tents. Wherever they stopped, the tents were set up in a large circle, in the center of which was the emperor's tent of yellow linen.

K'ang-hsi had invited the Mongols to meet him for a feast and entertainment. Ceremonial banners were flying and bright colored umbrellas shining in the sun as the wild warriors came riding up to the circle of tents. And there to receive them, surrounded by his mandarins in their long handsome robes, was their emperor in his robe of yellow satin embroidered with golden dragons. After the feast, K'ang-hsi pro-

vided his guests with the perfect kind of entertainment. He had them compete before him in horse races, wrestling and tricks on horseback in which they excelled. Appreciating and praising their great skill, he won their undying loyalty.

Next, on his return, K'ang-hsi traveled south through every province to see for himself that justice was being done and that nowhere in his empire did the people have any cause for rebellion. True to his name, peace was to be unbroken for

146

the remaining forty years of his reign. It would be remembered as a time of Lasting Peace.

During the war, Father Verbiest and the Jesuits had manufactured three hundred cannon for the emperor's use. Although the Chinese had invented gunpowder, they used it only for fireworks. They did not manufacture guns or cannon. To express his gratitude for their help, K'ang-hsi paid a visit to the house of the Jesuits, and as a gift for their church, he wrote the words "Honor God" in Chinese characters. This gave them added hope of converting the Chinese to the Catholic religion, which was their purpose in coming to China.

康熙

Now that the peaceful well-ordered days had returned, K'ang-hsi was able to resume his studies with Father Verbiest and to carry out some of the plans he had long had in mind. He had Chinese scholars begin work on a huge dictionary of the Chinese language, which is still the standard dictionary of China. Summoning both Chinese and Jesuit scholars he set them to work collecting the material for an encyclopedia that would contain both the wisdom of ancient China and the new sciences of western Europe.

東

(EAST)

RUSSIA

(IN ASIA)

北北
MONGOLS

·Nerchinsk

北
MANCHUS

AMUR RIVER

北

東

西
西
天下

Gobi Desert

THE GREAT WALL

·Peking

東

東

CHINA

JAPAN

南
南
東

Delhi·
Calcutta·

INDIA

·Taiwan

ASIA

THE YEAR THAT FATHER VERBIEST DIED, five Jesuit missionaries from France arrived in China, the first ones ever to come from France.

150

K'ang-hsi was away stag hunting in Mongolia when they reached Peking, but on his return he was delighted to see a painting of their King Louis XIV, which they had brought along, and to meet their leader, Father Gerbillon.

The first thing these five Frenchmen had to do was to learn to speak Chinese, which they must have done in a rather short time. For it was only a year later that K'ang-hsi sent Father Gerbillon and one of the others as interpreters to a most important meeting between Russia and China.

Here the Chinese delegation is passing through a gate in the Great Wall. For centuries this huge wall had protected China's northern border from invasion. But now the land belonging to China extended far beyond the Great Wall to the border of Russia. Russian traders had recently built a fort across the border line in the land of the Mongols, causing a disagreement that had to be settled. The meeting place was the town of Nerchinsk on the Amur River. There in 1689 Russia and China signed a treaty. This was the first treaty that China ever made with any European nation.

It took the Russians three years from the time they left Moscow until they reached the meeting place. There were two hundred and fifty in the party, headed by a young nobleman named Golovin, whose father was the governor general of Siberia.

The Chinese had erected a yellow linen tent for the meetings. On the appointed day, precisely on the hour, the Chinese approached, each mandarin dressed in his state robe of embroidered satin, preceded by officers carrying colorful umbrellas and imperial banners.

From the opposite direction, to the sound of fife and drums, came the Russians in their long cloaks lined with sable and their high pointed hats edged with fur. Inside the tent, the Russians and Chinese sat on two long benches facing one another. After elaborate greetings, they took up the business of the meeting. The interpreters translated what was said in either language into Latin. No agreement over the border line could be reached by the delegates that day or the next.

Father Gerbillon felt almost sure that with the vast amount of land the Russians already had, they did not want more land. What they actually wanted was to establish trade with China, to exchange their rich furs for porcelains and satins. Therefore, in a day or so, he went by himself to the tent of Golovin with a proposal. He promised that if the Russians would destroy their new fort and keep to the old boundary line, China would be willing to trade with them and give them a house for their headquarters in Peking. This proposal was accepted at once, and copied in Latin, Chinese and Russian so that each delegate could read the exact words.

All gathered again in their ceremonial costumes for the final meeting. Each holding a copy of the treaty took an oath in the name of his ruler that it would be faithfully observed. As a courtesy to the Russians, who were Christians, K'ang-hsi had suggested that the name of their Supreme God also be included.

Gifts were then exchanged—telescopes and a mirror given by the Russians, brocades and porcelains by the Chinese. Before dawn next day the tents were down and the delegates on their way home.

EVERY SPRING AND AUTUMN, K'ang-hsi paid a visit to the tomb of Confucius to perform ceremonies in his honor. Ever since his school days when he had first copied the laws of Confucius, K'ang-hsi had tried to follow them, especially the simple rule of life given to the two herdsmen:

DO NOT DO TO OTHERS WHAT YOU WOULD

NOT HAVE THEM DO TO YOU.

The Jesuits, for example, were his friends and had served him well. They had come to China to preach their religion.

154

Although it was not his religion, he believed they should be free to teach and preach, to build churches and make converts, so long as they respected the ancient beliefs and customs of China. The Jesuits saw no reason not to. Indeed they saw similarities in the teachings of Confucius with those found in the Bible. Jesus had given a similar Golden Rule for living:

DO UNTO OTHERS

AS YOU WOULD THEY SHOULD DO UNTO YOU.

Also, "honor thy father and thy mother" was one of the Ten Commandments.

In 1699, however, the Jesuits received an order from the Pope in Rome forbidding any Chinese Christian to attend any ceremony honoring either Confucius or their ancestors. The Jesuits were heartbroken. As for K'ang-hsi, he was shocked and amazed.

"Why," he said, "should one who knows nothing about the customs of China tell my people what to do? I would not presume to judge the customs of Europe of which I know nothing!"

The Jesuits sent a letter of protest to the Pope but it did no good. K'ang-hsi was patient for seventeen years. Then he issued an edict banishing all Christian missionaries, except astronomers and scholars. No one was allowed to teach the Christian religion. The churches they had built were turned into schools and town halls.

Eighty years before this, the shogun of Japan had driven out the Christian missionaries and also all the European traders, except the traders from Holland, who brought no missionaries with them. Dutch ships were allowed to come once a year to one small island. Otherwise Japan was closed to the world for over two hundred years. Toward the end of his reign, K'ang-hsi also became concerned about the European traders who were coming to China in greater numbers each year.

"The Europeans," he said to his ministers, "are bold and clever. They accomplish whatever they undertake. As long as I live, China has nothing to fear. But if the government became feeble, if we had civil war again or were invaded by the Mongols, the Europeans could do with China as they pleased."

In 1722, when he had reigned for sixty years, K'ang-hsi invited all the old men over sixty years of age to a joyous feast and celebration. The climax was a display of fireworks, giant firecrackers and rockets that burst into showers of falling stars, trees of green fire and dragons of brilliant red, the color of joy!

PART EIGHT

introducing

PETER THE GREAT

Tsar of Russia

who introduced western ideas to Russia

and placed his country among the

powerful nations of Europe

1682–1725

ПЕТРЬ

BELLS WERE RINGING! Thousands of bells from all the church towers in Moscow were clanging out a welcome to young Tsar Peter, who was entering his capital city for the first time as its absolute and undisputed ruler.

159

It was a fine day in October, 1689. Peter, who was to be known as Peter the Great, was seventeen years old. A handsome young giant on a prancing horse, he came riding into the city followed by a company of soldiers.

Red Square was crowded with people, and horses and riders went clattering through the market place and on over a moat into the huge old fortress known as the Kremlin, which was the heart of Moscow. There, in front of the royal palace, the soldiers came to a halt and dismounted. As they walked toward the entrance, Peter's head could be seen far above all the others, for he was nearly seven feet tall.

Peter had been born in the palace. When he was ten years old, his father had died and he had been made tsar with his mother as the regent, or ruler. Very soon, however, Peter's grown-up half sister Sofia had seized control of the government and had her own brother, Ivan, as well as Peter declared tsar. On days when the two boys held court, they sat on a double throne with a small prompting door in the back through which Sofia could tell them exactly what to do and say. Ivan was fifteen, but mentally retarded and unable to understand what was going on.

Ten-year-old Peter was very bright and strong but he wasn't

interested. He had more exciting things to think about, like guns and cannon! He could hardly wait to leave Moscow and get back to the country town where he and his mother lived, and where he kept an army of playmates engaged in a never-ending game of war.

It was not until he was seventeen that Peter ever flatly refused to do what Sofia told him to. This started a struggle between them that came to a climax on a night in August. Peter was awakened out of a sound sleep and told to flee for his life, for the Palace Guards sent out by Sofia were on their way to murder him.

This was a false alarm, but the terror of it gave Peter courage to stand up for his rights. Soon commanders of the Palace Guards, eager to be on the winning side, joined forces with Peter. Sofia, stripped of her power, was sent to a convent, where she was to be kept a prisoner for the rest of her life.

So that is how this glad day of celebration came about, when all the bells in Moscow were ringing and young Peter the Great was entering his capital city not as the tsar in name only but as the absolute ruler.

PETER STAYED IN MOSCOW NO LONGER than he had to. As soon as possible, he left ministers in charge of the government and went off to the country to build boats—actually build them with his own hands. He had been possessed with the idea of building boats ever since he had seen a sailboat for the first time. It was an old dilapidated boat which he had found while rummaging in a storehouse in the country. He had asked his Dutch tutor, who was with him, what it was

162

and how it worked. When he was told that without any oars it could travel against the wind, Peter could hardly believe it. The only boats to be seen in Russia were flat-bottomed barges loaded with furs or grain being poled along the rivers. This old sailboat, the Dutchman declared, had been made in England. Peter thought it might have been sent as a gift to one of his ancestors. Years later he was to call it the "grandfather of the Russian navy."

After the old ship had been repaired, Peter had it sent to a large lake about fifty miles north of Moscow where he arranged to have it copied. Huts were built for woodsmen and carpenters. Under the supervision of two Dutchmen they were soon cutting down trees and building the new ships.

It was to this lake that Peter was hurrying back after the trouble with Sofia was over. As soon as he got there, he put on workman's clothes and began helping the carpenters. All winter long he worked from dawn to dark at full speed, the way he did everything. Even after drinking and carousing most of the night, which he usually did, he was up again at dawn and ready for work.

As he worked beside the lake, he kept wondering what the sea and the great sea-going ships must be like. The only place to reach the sea was at Archangel. Archangel was Russia's only seaport, but its harbor was frozen nine months of the year. Peter reached it in early summer as the ice was melting and the first ships were coming in with merchandise from Holland and England. He decided at once that Russia should have a navy and immediately ordered a warship from Holland to be delivered to Archangel the following summer.

Yet if Russia was to have a navy, she must also have a seaport that was open all year, either on the Baltic Sea or the Black Sea. To gain such a harbor on the Baltic meant a war with Sweden; on the Black Sea it meant a war with Turkey. War with Turkey came first.

In the spring of 1695 a Russian army went south to capture the Turkish fortress of Azov. The Russians were utterly defeated. Peter was shocked, but he saw the reason for it. No army could ever capture the fort because the Turkish ships in the harbor kept it supplied with ammunition. In order to gain the harbor, Russia first had to capture the ships. At least twenty-five warships would be needed, over one thousand barges and smaller ships. All must be built during the winter and be ready for spring.

Peter didn't know the word impossible, so he plunged ahead with plans and preparations. He sent to Archangel to have the warship he had ordered from Holland taken apart to be used as a pattern. Every part was numbered and sent to a town near the Don River where the navy was to be built. By rounding up laborers and carpenters by the thousands and forcing them to work for sixteen hours a day, the impossible was accomplished. The ships were built, and before the end of July, the Turkish fortress of Azov had been captured. Russia had her harbor on the Black Sea and Peter returned to Moscow in triumph.

As usual he did not stay long in Moscow. By spring of the following year he was off on a visit to Europe.

THE PEOPLE OF WESTERN EUROPE, of England, France, Holland and the other countries, did not think of Russia as being part of Europe. To them it was a big backward land called Muscovy which had been ruled for two hundred years by the Mongols.

The Russians, for the most part, were satisfied to be as they were. They took no interest in Europe and distrusted all Europeans. Those who came to Moscow were obliged to live in the

Foreign Quarter, apart from the rest of the city. The old Boyars, or noblemen, especially disliked and disapproved of the foreigners. Their clothes were tight and ugly. And worse, they defied the Lord by shaving their faces, knowing full well that God intended men to have beards.

Peter disagreed with these "Old Believers." Whenever he was in Moscow, he spent much time in the Foreign Quarter, talking with his European friends. The more he heard about Europe, the more eager he became to see for himself what Russia needed to know. He lost no time after his return from the war in organizing a group to go with him on a European journey. Anyone who objected to this got a taste of the tsar's violent temper. One Old Believer was knocked down by a single blow of Peter's huge fist and then taken off to be beaten with a rope.

On March 9, 1697, the group of travelers, known as the Grand Embassy, left for the west—over two hundred people in all, counting servants, clowns, drummers, trumpeters, outriders and guards. Peter did not want to be recognized and stared at, so he appointed one of his European friends to head the delegation. He himself went in workman's clothes, pretending to be a carpenter. The disguise was a failure. Being almost seven feet tall he was spotted everywhere as being the tsar of Russia.

Otherwise his visit to Europe was a great success. In Holland he worked as a ship's carpenter, first on the docks at Zaandam and later at Amsterdam in the shipyards of the East India Company. From there he went to meet the Dutchman, William III, who was the king of England, and who was then in Holland for an international meeting. William III invited the tsar and his embassy to visit England and provided ships to take them there.

Peter spent four months in England, working in the royal shipyards at Deptford, where it was said "he worked as hard with his hands as any man in the yard." He also went everywhere in and around London to see and learn everything possible to carry back with him to Russia.

In the Tower of London he inspected the latest types of guns and cannon. At the Royal Mint he admired the new silver coins designed by Isaac Newton, who had recently given up teaching at Cambridge to become Master of the Mint. At the Greenwich Observatory he discussed astronomy and mathematics with the royal astronomers. At Oxford he was presented with several books on mathematics.

One Sunday in April, he attended the Quaker meeting in Deptford and spent the afternoon discussing Quaker beliefs with Mr. William Penn, who had come to pay him a visit. The tsar was most interested in the Friend's ideas but he questioned whether Quakers were any use to their country when they refused to carry arms or to fight. He was glad to receive the Quaker books William Penn brought for him, translated

into Dutch, the only foreign language Peter knew.

Three weeks later, Peter's visit to England was over and he went away, leaving behind memories of himself that ranged from brilliant and charming to crude and disgusting. At Deptford the Russians occupied the fine house of an English lord, which they left badly damaged from their rowdy drunken parties. The government had to send Sir Christopher Wren, the architect, the figure out what the owner must be paid to replace all the broken windows, ruined floors and furniture.

Peter sailed away on the *Royal Transport,* a beautiful yacht, which was a gift from King William. It was manned by an English crew who were to sail it from Amsterdam to Archangel as soon as the ice melted.

Peter also chartered ten other ships to carry back the vast quantity of arms, equipment and scientific instruments he had purchased, as well as the hundreds of officers, engineers and skilled artisans he had hired to teach Russian workmen how to use the new machinery.

Peter had planned to visit Vienna and Venice on the way home, but at Vienna he had bad news that sent him speeding back to Moscow as fast as he could ride.

THE PALACE GUARDS HAD REVOLTED AGAINST HIM! When he arrived in Moscow his frenzy of pent-up terror and wrath exploded with the fury of a raging volcano. The Palace Guards were utterly destroyed. One by one, two thousand guards were dragged to Red Square and beheaded. To begin with, Peter took the ax in his own hands and chopped off the heads. As soon as the bloody deed was completed he replaced the guards with soldiers he could trust, and gave his attention to his one great project—the modernizing of Russia.

THIS OLD CARTOON SHOWS PETER with a pair of shears cutting off a nobleman's beard. Getting rid of beards was the first of Peter's many changes. All the changes were resented by the Old Believers, but none more than being obliged to part with their long beards. Being forced to give up their long robes was the next insult. Barbers and tailors were stationed at the city gates to shave everyone who passed or measure him for a new suit. Later on, a man who insisted on keeping his beard might do so by paying a "beard tax."

JANUARY, 1700: All the first week of that month Peter kept the nights of Moscow bright with fireworks and bonfires. This was to celebrate not merely a new year and a new century but a new calendar, another reform bitterly opposed by the Old Believers. Instead of using their old familiar calendar which counted the years from the Creation of the World, they must now use a strange European calendar which took the Birth of Christ as Year One. That turned the old year 7208 into the year 1700. What was even more shocking, each year began in January instead of September. That was not only immoral, argued the Old Believers, it was impossible according to the Bible. How, in the Garden of Eden, could the serpent who tempted Eve have found an apple in January? It had to be in September when the apples were ripe!

Peter had no time to worry about apples. He had too many more important projects on his mind.

BY SUMMER, PETER HAD STARTED his great Northern
War against Sweden, in order to gain a harbor for Russia on
the Baltic Sea. The king of Sweden, Charles XII, who was a
brilliant young warrior, defeated the Russians in the first battle. But then he suddenly turned aside to fight against Poland,
which gave Russia a chance to capture land at the mouth of
the Neva River.

There in the spring of 1703 Peter began building a small log fort which soon grew into the town of Petersburg. Later it became his capital city and in honor of his patron saint he named it St. Petersburg.

It was a wretched place to choose for a city. The Neva branches into four main muddy streams, leaving nothing but marshy islands in between. The weather was so damp and cold that thousands of workmen died even before the foundations were completed. Piles had to be sunk into the marsh first. Earth was so scarce that the men had to carry it from a great distance in their long tunics or in bags made of rags. Wheelbarrows were unknown and spades and picks were so scarce the men often had to scrape up the soil with their hands. Over two hundred thousand died turning that swamp into dry land. People began to say it was the lime in their bones that hardened the soil.

The first summer Peter lived in a small log house built in two days. When the Neva flooded, the water on the floor stood over a foot deep. But he loved the whole place and called it "Paradise." Someday, he believed, his city would be as beautiful as Amsterdam, which was also built on islands and canals. He sent to Holland for a Dutch architect to design the buildings. He imported printing presses and started the first Russian newspaper, the *Gazette* of St. Petersburg.

By 1712 he had become so excited over his new city that he decided to make it the capital. Unlike Moscow, with its old-fashioned ways, St. Petersburg could be made a center of western civilization—"a window to Europe."

St. Petersburg was the capital of Russia until 1917 when the Russian Revolution turned the empire of the tsars into the Union of Soviet Socialist Republics. Honoring a hero of the revolution, Peter's city became Leningrad.

To be his capital city, Peter decided that unlike old Moscow, which was made entirely of wood, St. Petersburg should be built of stone. Since there was not a single stone to be seen in that marshy land, he quickly issued a decree to solve the problem. Every nobleman was obliged to leave his estate, bring stones with him and build himself a house of stone in St. Petersburg.

During these years of building, Peter was gone much of the time fighting the war against Sweden. The war lasted for twenty years, during which the Russian army invaded Sweden three times. Finally, when the treaty was signed, Peter had far more than he set out to win. Not only did he have his port on the Baltic but all of Sweden's Baltic provinces. On the day he returned to St. Petersburg bells rang, drums rolled, trumpets sounded and in a formal ceremony he was hailed as Father of his Fatherland and also given the title

PETER THE GREAT.

Two years later the little old boat which had started it all was brought to St. Petersburg, placed in the water and saluted with cannon fire as the "grandfather of the Russian Navy."

Peter died in 1725. Like a great giant, he had dragged Russia out of the dark ages into the modern world and made it one of the powerful nations of Europe. Yet the Old Believers were glad to see him go. This old popular cartoon shows them as Mice burying the dead Cat.

PART NINE

concluding the life story of

WILLIAM PENN

1699–1718

telling of his second visit to

PENNSYLVANIA

why he stayed only two years

and how his life ended in

ENGLAND

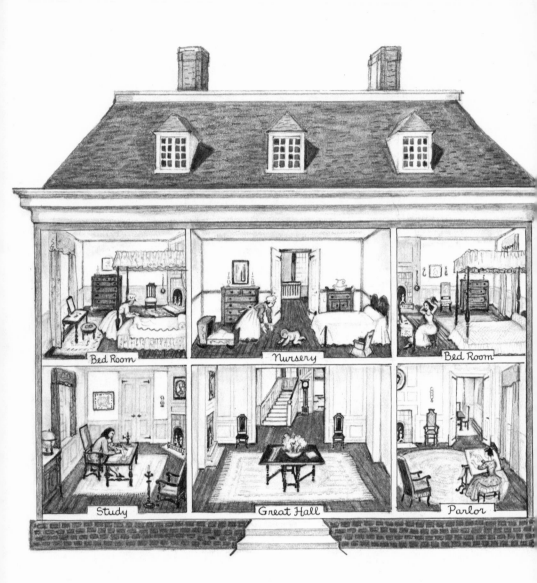

Bed Room

Nursery

Bed Room

Study

Great Hall

Parlor

PENNSBURY MANOR

1699

Hannah Penn + James Logan

AT LONG LAST IN SEPTEMBER, 1699, the year after his meeting with Peter the Great, William Penn sailed for America. Expecting never to return, he sent ashore from the ship a letter of final farewell to the Quakers of England, Holland and elsewhere in Europe.

Of the three small children to whom he had written farewell letters before his first voyage, only Letitia was with him. She was now twenty-one. William Junior, who had grown into a wild extravagant fellow, had married and at nineteen was about to become a father. Springett, the oldest, a fine young man whom his father had counted on for help and support, had died soon after his mother.

Two other young people, however, had now entered the life of William Penn. They were to be devoted to him as long as he lived. One was his new wife, Hannah Callowhill Penn, twenty years younger than her husband. The other was his new secretary, James Logan, a young Scotsman born in Ireland, who was both a brilliant student and a capable business man.

The voyage took almost three months. As soon as his ship was sighted, settlers and Indians crowded the shore to catch a glimpse of the great William Penn they had heard so much about but never seen. It was no disappointment as they saw him step ashore and in his elegant courtly manner greet those who had come to welcome him. And what a joy it was for William Penn to see Philadelphia, his beloved city! How it had grown in the years he had been gone! It now had a population of five thousand and next to Boston was the largest city in the colonies. Along its broad streets were seven hundred brick houses all surrounded by wide lawns and beautiful gardens.

It was planned that the Penn family should spend the winter in what was called the "Slate Roof House," where they could live in the elegant way suited to the governor of so prosperous a province. There on January 28, 1700, John Penn was born, the only one of William Penn's children to be born in America.

As soon as summer came, the family moved from Philadelphia to the lovely country home of Pennsbury, twenty-five miles up the river by boat. Letitia helped Hannah manage a large staff of servants and entertain the many guests who came to enjoy the governor's hospitality.

From the day he arrived, William Penn followed a strenuous program of work. His greatest problem was trying to keep peace between the two hostile groups into which the colony had become divided—the Quakers and the non-Quakers. Most of the non-Quakers belonged to the Church of England.

Another problem was to capture and punish the many pirates who sailed along the coast, seizing and plundering British ships before they reached the harbor. All the English colonies from Massachusetts to Virginia suffered from the pirates. The most famous pirate, Captain Kidd, had recently been arrested in New York and sent to England for trial.

There were many other dangers and problems that the colonies shared. Most of them, William Penn believed, could be handled far better if the colonies were united. In early fall, he invited the governors of Massachusetts, New York and Virginia to meet and talk with him about a plan he had for uniting the colonies. The governors readily agreed to his plan for union, and it was sent to England to be considered by the king's Privy Council. It could hardly have arrived at a worse time. The Council could think of nothing but the war about to be declared against France—another war started by Louis XIV, the lifelong enemy of William III. It was called the War of the Spanish Succession. This is how it began: The king of Spain had died, leaving no son to inherit the throne, so Louis XIV immediately claimed the throne for his grandson, Philip V, whose Spanish grandmother (as shown on the family chart) was Maria Theresa. In that way Louis XIV would gain control of Spain and all of Spain's vast territory in the New World.

As William Penn knew only too well, war in Europe between France and England meant war between the French and English in America. And if Pennsylvania did not furnish enough military aid, the province might be taken away from him again and placed under a royal governor appointed by the king. What made this even more probable was the fact that one of his enemies in the colony had been sending complaints about him to the Privy Council. There seemed nothing to do but return to London and defend himself, leaving James Logan to look after his interests in Pennsylvania.

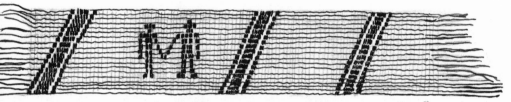

INDIAN BELT OF WAMPUM GIVEN TO "BROTHER ONUS"

The Indians, hearing that their good friend "Brother Onus" was leaving, came to say farewell and repeat their faith in the old Treaty of Peace. As proof of this, one chieftain stepped forward, placed his hand to his head, then struck his heart three times to show that true covenants were made not with the head but with the heart. This is the treasured belt of wampum which the Indians had given their good friend when the Great Treaty was signed.

William Penn had wanted Hannah to remain at Pennsbury with "Tishe" and "little Johnne" until he returned, but she refused. So the family went with him. It was well that they did, for on November 3, 1701, when William Penn sailed from Pennsylvania, he saw his province for the last time.

DUM·CLAVUM·TENEAM

William Penn Esq. Proprietor
of Pensylvania. 1703

WILLIAM PENN'S FIRST LETTER to James Logan from England told of his great distress due to lack of money. "Hasten over rents etc.," he wrote, "all that thou canst . . . I am forced to borrow money and add debt to debt instead of paying them . . . My wife is kept by her father. . . ." (He could not even afford to have Hannah join him in London.)

James Logan did his best. As actual money was scarce in America, he began to ship beer, flour, pork, tobacco and furs to be sold in England. But war soon made that impossible. English ships were being seized by France.

Meanwhile William Penn's debts and expenses kept on mounting. Letitia's newly wed husband was clamoring for her unpaid dowry. William Junior was running up one bill after another for his long-suffering father to pay.

Worst of all was Penn's long-standing debt to a man named Ford, who had been his secretary for thirty years. Ford had continually presented William Penn with bills for money supposedly spent in his employer's behalf. And William Penn, trusting him completely but unable to pay the money, had given Ford a mortgage on thousands of acres in Pennsylvania.

Now the Ford family threatened to sell all that Pennsylvania land if Penn did not pay them 11,000 pounds in six months. Six months passed and the Fords increased the amount he owed them to 14,000 pounds.

One Sunday, bailiffs acting for the Fords burst into the Friends Meeting House and tried to arrest William Penn for debt. They did not succeed, but a few hours later, William Penn went by himself to the debtor's prison.

To have such a dreadful thing happen to this great Friend so shocked the Quakers that they quickly came to his aid. As they examined the Fords' bookkeeping and the bills William Penn had so trustfully signed, they were even more shocked to see how badly Ford had cheated him. Even the royal treasurer felt sympathetic toward Penn and reduced by almost one half the amount he was to pay the Fords. This amount was provided by several Quakers, to whom William Penn gave new mortgages on his Pennsylvania property.

It was then 1708. During most of those miserable poverty-stricken years, Hannah had lived with her father. Finally, after much looking and many disappointments, William Penn was able to find a home for his family. It was a large house in the country west of London on the way to Oxford. There with his devoted Hannah and their five children, happy busy years passed by until the fall of 1712.

On the fourth of October, as William Penn sat at his desk writing a letter to James Logan, the writing suddenly stopped, his hand paralyzed by a stroke that left him unconscious. Although he partially recovered and lived for another six years, his thoughts were blurred, his memory gone. So that October day when the quill dropped from his hand marked the end of his active life. It was the closing page of the history which he helped to write, and so brings to an end this story of the World of William Penn.

INDEX

Entries referring to people are set in boldface type.

189

Germany, 91, 131
Glorious Revolution (England), 129
Golden Rule, 44, 137–38, 155
Golovin, Russian nobleman, 152–53
Great Plague, 17, 105
Greenwich (time), 115
Griffin, The, 67, 68. *See also* La Salle

Hall of Mirrors, 84–85
Halley, Edmund, 116–20
Halley's Comet, 119–20
Holland, 81, 89, 90–92, 128, 131. *See also* William
Holy Experiment, 36, 44. *See also* Pennsylvania; Penn, William
Huygens, Christian, Dutch scientist, 108

Illinois River, 68, 70
India, 92, 95–100
Indians, American: and William Penn, 44–48, 185; language of, 48; location of, 69; Illinois, 60–62, 68; Arkansas, 62–63
Ireland, 23–24, 128, 130
Ivan, tsar of Russia, 160

James, duke of York (later James II, king of England), 14, 40–41, 51, 125–28, 130
Jesuits: in New France, 56, 58; in China, 140, 142, 147, 150–51, 153–56. *See also* Marquette, Père
Jolliet, Louis, 58–63

Kang-hsi, emperor of China: youth, 135–38; and teachings of Confucius, 137–38, 144, 154–55; as a scholar, 137–42, 147; and the Jesuits, 140, 142, 147, 151, 154–56; as soldier and ruler, 143–47, 151, 153, 156

Kidd, Captain, 183

La Salle, Robert Cavelier, Sieur de, 63–68, 70
La Vallière, Louise, 79, 84
Leeuwenhoek, Anton van, 121–22
Logan, James, secretary to William Penn, 182, 185, 186, 188
London, 21–22
London, great fire of, 18–20, 22, 96
London, Tower of, 27–28, 169
Lord Baltimore, 33, 37, 50–52
Louis XIV, king of France: and Cardinal Mazarin, 74–76; assumes power, 77–81; marries, 76, 79; Sun King, 79, 80, 85; and Versailles, 81–82, 84–86, 108; wages war, 81, 89–92, 126, 128, 130–31, 184; and arts and science; 87–88, 108
Louis the Great. *See* Louis XIV
Louisiana, 70

Magna Carta, 29
Manchu dynasty, 135–36, 138. *See also* K'ang-hsi
Mansart, architect, 84
Maria Theresa, queen of France, 76, 79, 88
Markham, William, cousin of William Penn, 37, 44
Marquette, Père, 58–60, 62–63
Mary, daughter of James II (later Mary II, queen of England), 127–29, 132
Maryland, 33, 37, 50–52
Massachusetts, 32–33, 184
Mazarin, Cardinal, 74–77
"Merry Monarch." *See* Charles II
Ming dynasty, 136
Mississippi River, 57–60, 62, 63, 70
Missouri River, 62

190

Mogul dynasty, 95, 97–100. *See also* India

Molière, 86–88

Mongols, 143–46, 167

Montespan, Madame de, 90

Moscow, 158–60, 167–68, 172, 174, 177

Moslem religion, 97, 99

Neva River, 175–76

New Castle (Delaware), 11, 40

New France, 56, 64, 65, 131, 132

Newgate Prison, 30

New Jersey, 33

Newton, Sir Isaac: youth and education of, 103–5; scientific discoveries of, 109–13, 120; at Cambridge, 112–13, 169; writes the *Principia,* 118

New York, 52, 132, 184

Ohio River, 62, 64

Old Believers, 168, 173–74, 178. *See also* Peter the Great

Oxford University, 14–16

Palace Guards, 161, 172

Paris, 81, 88

Paris Observatory, 108, 113, 115, 120

Parliament (English), 13, 17, 76, 129

Parliament (French), 75

Penn, Gulielma Springett (first wife), 31, 33, 38, 39, 125, 132

Penn, Hannah Callowhill (second wife), 182–83, 185, 186, 188

Penn, John (son), 183, 185

Penn, Letitia (daughter), 39, 181, 183, 185, 186

Penn, Springett (son), 39, 181

Penn, William, 8–11: youth and education of, 13–17; becomes a Quaker, 17, 23–26, 27–30; marries,

31; as governor of New Jersey, 33–34; acquires Delaware and Pennsylvania, 34–37; visits America, 38–42; and the Indians, 44–48, 185; writes Great Law, 49–50; and border dispute, 50–52; returns to England, 52, 125; and Royal Society, 117; and James II, 126, 127, 130; and William III, 132; and Peter the Great, 170; visits America again, 181–83; back to England, 184–85; last years, 186–88

Penn, William Jr. (son), 39, 181, 187

Penn, Sir William (father), 13–16, 19, 23–26, 28, 30, 126

Pennsbury Manor, 42, 43, 180, 183

Pennsylvania, 9–11, 33–37, 49–52, 130, 184–85, 187–88

Pepys, Samuel, 14, 16, 19–20, 108, 118

Peter the Great, tsar of Russia: the young ruler, 159–61; and the navy, 162–64, 166; and war with Turkey, 164, 166; visits Europe, 166–71; puts down revolt, 172; and Old Believers, 168, 173–74; and war with Sweden, 175, 177–78; builds St. Petersburg, 176–78; death, 178

Philadelphia, 9–10, 36–37, 42, 182

Phillip, king of Spain, 90

Pirates, 183

Principia, 118. *See also* Newton, Sir Isaac

Puritans, 13, 32–33

Quakers: persecution of, 11, 17, 27, 32–33, 126; beliefs of 24–25, 132, 170; origin of name, 32; in the New World, 34, 132, 183, 188

Religious persecution, 11, 17, 27, 32–33, 126
Royal Observatory, 115
Royal Society of London, 107–8, 110, 117–18, 121–22
Russia, 151–53, 163–64, 166–68, 172–78. *See also* Peter the Great

Saint Paul's Cathedral, 22
Saint Petersburg, 176–78
Shackamaxon, 46
Shah Jahan, emperor of India, 95–97
Sofia, half-sister to Peter the Great, 160, 161
Spain, 90–92, 131, 184
Spanish Succession, War of the, 184
Sun King, 80, 85. *See also* Louis XIV
Sweden, 90, 131, 175, 177–78

Taj Mahal, 94–96
Tower Hill, 15, 16, 19
Turkey, 164, 166

Verbiest, Father Ferdinand, Jesuit priest in China, 140–42, 147, 150
Versailles, 81–86, 108
Virginia, 184
Voltaire, 48

Welcome (ship), 10, 40
West New Jersey, 33–34, 37
William, Prince of Orange (later William III, king of England), 90–92, 128–32, 169, 171, 184
Wren, Sir Christopher, 21–22, 107, 115, 171